The Thinking University Expanded

The Thinking University Expanded considers how the university can be extended and developed into an institution of play that becomes a gateway to new compositions and enactments of opportunities and happiness for university academics and students alike. A university of and in continuous play can shape the public sphere in ways that reimagine both the epistemological and the political, and the metaphysical and the ethical.

Without abandoning the university's emphasis on thinking, the book examines the prospects of opening the university to 'a new, possible use'. The singular outcomes-based lens of seeing higher education distorts the humane and ethical nuance of what a university can potentially do and aspire towards. For this reason, the book intends to find a new use for the idea of a university – one that is responsible and responsive in both its pursuit of the truth and being open to different kinds of truth, as made manifest in diverse contexts and life-worlds.

This book will be of great interest for academics, researchers and postgraduate students in the field of higher education.

Yusef Waghid reads Philosophy of Education at Stellenbosch University. He is the editor-in-chief of *South African Journal of Higher Education* and principal editor of *Citizenship Teaching and Learning*, South Africa.

Nuraan Davids is Professor of Philosophy of Education at the Faculty of Education, Stellenbosch University, South Africa.

Routledge Research in Higher Education

The Tenure-Track Process for Chicana and Latina Faculty
Experiences of Resisting and Persisting in the Academy
Edited by Patricia A. Pérez

Higher Education in Nepal
Policies and Perspectives
Edited by Krishna Bista, Shyam Sharma, and Rosalind Latiner Raby

Race, Law, and Higher Education in the Colorblind Era
Critical Investigations into Race-Related Supreme Court Disputes
Hoang Vu Tran

Post-Recession Community College Reform
A Decade of Experimentation
Chet Jordan and Anthony G. Picciano

Building Soft Skills for Employability
Challenges and Practices in Vietnam
Tran Le Huu Nghia

Life for the Academic in the Neoliberal University
Alpesh Maisuria and Svenja Helmes

The Doctorate Experience in Europe and Beyond
Supervision, Languages, Identities
Michael Byram and Maria Stoicheva

For more information about this series, please visit: www.routledge.com/Routledge-Research-in-Higher-Education/book-series/RRHE

The Thinking University Expanded
On Profanation, Play and Education

Yusef Waghid and Nuraan Davids

LONDON AND NEW YORK

First published 2020
by Routledge
2 Park Square, Milton Park, Abingdon, Oxon OX14 4RN

and by Routledge
52 Vanderbilt Avenue, New York, NY 10017

Routledge is an imprint of the Taylor & Francis Group, an informa business

First issued in paperback 2021

© 2020 Yusef Waghid & Nuraan Davids

The right of Yusef Waghid and Nuraan Davids to be identified as authors of this work has been asserted by him/her/them in accordance with sections 77 and 78 of the Copyright, Designs and Patents Act 1988.

All rights reserved. No part of this book may be reprinted or reproduced or utilised in any form or by any electronic, mechanical, or other means, now known or hereafter invented, including photocopying and recording, or in any information storage or retrieval system, without permission in writing from the publishers.

Trademark notice: Product or corporate names may be trademarks or registered trademarks, and are used only for identification and explanation without intent to infringe.

British Library Cataloguing-in-Publication Data
A catalogue record for this book is available from the British Library

Library of Congress Cataloging-in-Publication Data
A catalog record has been requested for this book

ISBN: 978-0-367-43208-9 (hbk)
ISBN: 978-1-03-208348-3 (pbk)
ISBN: 978-1-003-00185-0 (ebk)

Typeset in Times New Roman
by codeMantra

Contents

Foreword   vi
Preface   x

1. The thinking university reconsidered   1
2. On searching for truth and the justification for telling the truth   14
3. Student alienation and the democratic mission of a university re-examined   25
4. On some of the limitations of citizenship and the thinking university   37
5. Towards a university beyond critique   47
6. On a university without condition   57
7. Against the exclusive entrepreneurial university   66
8. Al-Rumi and the notion of a university beyond critique   78
9. An argument in defence of a playful university   89
10. On a university in perpetual play   100

Index   110

Foreword

Perhaps ever since its incarnation, and even before its inception in mediaeval times to its earlier formations in India, Persia and China, the university has been understood as a place of thought. In modern times – that is, over the past two hundred years or so, with the emergence of the Kantian university of reason – the university also came to be understood as a place for systematic inquiry and then of critique. Critique, after all, is not just thought but thought turned upon itself. But here, in this book, we are invited to think the unthinkable, of the university as being *beyond critique*.

Depending on one's point of view, this is either scandalous or question begging. It is scandalous because the idea of the university beyond critique seems to fire a torpedo into what, for many, lies at the heart of the university, which is its powers not just to examine all the entities in the universe but also to examine critically the categories and processes through which those enquiries gain their legitimacy. It is question begging because it seems to presume that the university is assuredly a place of critique. Of late, that the university is a place of thought has to be doubted, and on several fronts, not least with the rise across the world of populism, with instances coming to light of malpractices within the academic community (of data manipulation and of plagiarism) and increasing pressures on academics to publish, whatever the cost in profundity or originality. The idea of the university as being beyond critique will be awkward for some, especially for those who see critique as the *sine qua non* of the university and of that very feature of the university being under attack.

And yet, this book presses just that thought – that the idea of the university as a site of thought and of critique should itself be a subject of critical reflection. The suggestion here is that we may properly entertain the idea of a university beyond critique. The key here is that 'beyond', which is nicely ambiguous. 'Beyond' can mean leaving something behind, and perhaps going to another place entirely. (The explorer alighted on a place but then went on, well beyond it, and arrived at a quite different place.) It may, however, also mean encompassing an earlier position while also reaching a separate place. (In her journey towards becoming a concert pianist, our artist won the competition by going well beyond what might have been expected.) And it is surely that latter sense of 'beyond' that Waghid and Davids are opening to us here. We should retain – and, if necessary, regain – a sense of critique being a key concept for the university, but the university should be prepared to go well beyond critique; the university should not be limited by the idea of critique.

This is a radical idea – that the university goes beyond critique, but it is surely necessary for the university in the twenty-first century. It is not too much to say that the world is in peril, both in its general state as planet Earth and in its particulars – in extremism, anti-democratic populisms, extreme forms of vindictiveness, cross-state rivalries, technological surveillance, economic collapses, energy crises and so on. The university is doubly implicated in all of this. Firstly, it has spawned technologies and knowledge resources that have fuelled much of this – and, hence, lies behind the emergence of 'cognitive capitalism' (Boutang, 2011).

Secondly, the university is entangled with the world *discursively*. A dramatic example has recently been furnished by the United Kingdom, which held a referendum in 2016 as to whether it should remain a member of the European Union (an association of 27 European states) or whether it should leave. The result revealed a sharp division among the voters (with a 52%–48% vote in favour of 'leaving'). It turned out that the decisive influence in the voting preference lay not in social class or age or ethnicity or gender but in whether a voter had or had not experienced higher education (with those who had not experienced higher education largely voting to leave). The university, accordingly, is caught up in what can fairly be said to be a culture war – between those who have, and those who have not, experienced higher education living in quite different worlds and having markedly different holds on life.

The university, it can now accordingly be said, swims in difficult waters. An unwitting by-product of a combination of factors – especially the emergence of mass higher education, the rise of populism and an internet age of communication – is that the university is entangled with a discursive schism in society. In these circumstances, it is evident that knowledge, truth, understanding, thought and even critique are insufficient categories through which to do justice to the responsibilities now befalling the university. The university has to go beyond critique. This is not to abandon categories of knowledge, truth, understanding, thought and critique but to step beyond them.

But where and how? No line is sure; no method is entirely reliable. Accordingly, to deploy a further key idea of Waghid and Davids, this going beyond critique should include a measure of *play*. 'Play' conjures connotations of the theatre and the plays that are performed there, of games that are played, of light-heartedness and non-seriousness, and a lack of commitment and of a merely temporary move (as in 'playing the market') and of inauthenticity. However, this play is none of those. Rather, it is play in the sense of attempting, venturing, trying and experimenting. This would be a play in the sense of seeing how much 'play' there might be in the systems in which the university moves. It would be a play very much with intent, with determination on the part of the university.

Here, in our example, responsibilities are surely opening for the university to explore possibilities for it to help to forge a new kind of public sphere, *playing* its part in enabling citizens to comprehend and address complex issues (say, of ecological disturbance). For instance, around the world, various kinds of citizen forums are being established in connection with large and controversial issues, and surely, the university has a part to contribute here, playing with different arrangements in their structure, communication opportunities, styles and forms of outcome.

Such a reconsideration of the university in and for the twenty-first century would justifiably remove any lingering sacredness it might possess. In view is a *profanation* – to draw on another large idea here – that exposes the university to the world. No longer should the university content itself with its activities being framed in rather narrow, and largely interior, interests. It would be a profanation of the university, too, in which its educative function was extended to the world and in which it would entangle itself still further in the discourses of the world, with all the messiness that such a venture would harbour. Crucial in all of this, lastly, is an *ethics of shame*, in which such proposals carry with them a critique of the university itself, and so care needs to be taken in voicing such ideas. The university is not to be put in the dock for any alleged wrongdoing on its part but rather to be gently encouraged to take an even wider view of its responsibilities and possibilities in a troubled world.

Here, in this book, Yusef Waghid and Nuraan Davids open up these issues and do so in an open and conversational way that provides resources for yet further investigations, as they themselves would hope for. After all, the university envisaged here would be in perpetual play, and there can be no limit to the participants in this play.

Reference

Boutang, Y.-M. 2011. *Cognitive capitalism*. Cambridge: Polity.

Ronald Barnett
London, May 2019

Preface

Any intimation that a thinking university be expanded implicitly leads to other kinds of questions: on the one hand, expanded in relation to what or to whom, and, on the other hand, whether conceiving of a university as thinking is, in fact, a constraining endeavour. Stated differently, is the idea of a thinking university a sufficient condition for framing the idea of a university? Of course, we are not denying that 'the university is a thinking institution' (Barnett & Bengtsen, 2018: 1). It is impossible to dislocate the university from its epistemological imperative, and hence conceptions of thinking. It would appear, however, amidst neoliberal texts and contexts, that – to a large extent – universities have begun to undermine their own understandings of what constitutes a thinking university. Instead, what has become more pronounced are the slippages into metaphorical guises of university *performativity* – as in 'fitness for purpose', transformation of education', quality provision' and 'community engagement' – metaphors, which have somehow presumed the uncontested enabling conditions for a university to enact its role in society.

Recently, and coinciding with its centenary year, the university, where we are based, has once again reiterated its ambition towards intensive research excellence, coupled with an awareness of our institutional relevance and responsiveness to events in the world. On the surface, these two objectives are, of course, not mutually exclusive. It seems wholly reasonable to expect epistemological advancement, without an abandonment of social relevance and responsibility. We cannot lose sight, however, that the renewed commitment of our university to this duality of purpose unfolds in very performative ways and in ways that invariably get lost in tensions between performativity and neglect, and between proficiency and mediocrity.

Without abandoning a university's emphasis on thinking, we want to examine the possibility of opening up a university to 'a new, possible use', or what Giorgio Agamben refers to as the quest for profanation (Agamben, 2010: 85). How might the idea of a thinking university adopt yet-to-be-explored formations and relationships, so that it becomes possible for a university to think of itself beyond discovering truth and enhancing democracy, citizenship, critique and social justice? How can the idea of a thinking university manifest in ways that extend beyond traditional conceptions and expectations of academic performance and social impact? Our interest in this book, therefore, is to consider and imagine how a university can be expanded to an institution of play that can become a gateway to new compositions and enactments of opportunities and happiness for university academics and students alike.

We have outlined our approach in tackling the notion of a university of play as follows:

In Chapter 1, we employ the notion of a thinking university by examining, firstly, what constitutes the idea of a thinking university and, secondly, how the notion of a thinking university should organise its practices. We specifically accentuate the idea of antagonism in relation to a university's thinking and argue why a thinking university should take risks in realising its sense of openness, potentiality and hope.

Chapter 2 brings into question the idea of searching for truth in a thinking university. We use Derridian – that is, in relation to the seminal thoughts of French philosopher Jacques Derrida – understandings of deconstruction, justice and education to delineate tasks of a university, in particular being responsive to the otherness of others, being concerned with an openness to the immeasurable and incalculable and looking out for an impossible invention of the other – all aspects of what a thinking university should be doing. We extend the idea of a thinking university into the one that acts in relation to truth. Specifically, we are interested in a university which not only searches for truth but also 'tells the truth' – that is to act with reasonable justification. Likewise, we are interested in exploring the argument that in being both responsible and responsive, the university ought to be focused on nurturing and guiding students who are best equipped to address their own truths and those of others.

Chapter 3 takes into consideration an exposition of the democratic mission of a thinking university, as an instance of how such a university should play its role. For us, democratically radicalising a thinking university invokes actions of summoning teachers and students to speak their minds and provoking them to proffer plausible judgements and to act in attention of a university based on practices of equality, dissensus and a disturbance of doubts. If a university is to foster openness, where divergent points of view are brought into play, then this implies being willing to listen to and engage with radical ways of thinking and being.

In Chapter 4, we bring into contestation the idea of a thinking university in terms of the responsibility of cultivating a democratic citizenry. In doing so, we firstly and specifically take a closer look at why and how the public responsibility of a university can be linked to enabling a renewed attention on democratic citizenship. Secondly, we show how the cultivation of democratic citizenship seems to be commensurable with the idea of producing a thinking university. Thirdly, we identify some of the limitations of democratic citizenship, in particular its emphasis on patriotism, which can undermine any defensible form of a thinking university.

In Chapter 5, we engage, firstly, with the notion of a university of critique, as an instance of a thinking university. In doing so, we offer two accounts of a thinking university: one in which discomfort and restiveness prevail, and another in which dissensus and unsettlement hold sway. We argue that these two complementary accounts of critique corroborate thinking provoked from *outside* of university teachers and students. We argue in favour of a university of thinking along the lines of critique, and we want to examine how such a thinking university would look like beyond the realm of critique. That is, instead of just focusing on the presence of those *outside* of a university's thinking, we hold that looking *inside* of the self makes us attentive to the idea of bearing witness to the self and others – an idea that takes an understanding of a university of thinking beyond critique towards a new use. In a different way, this chapter touches on the idea of a university in profanation.

Chapter 6 introduces the idea of a university without condition. In our view, a university that draws on both critique and witnessing to carve out its professional path seems to be closely connected to what Jacques Derrida (2004: 11) expounds on in his fascinating contribution, 'The future of the profession or the unconditional university'. To Derrida, the university is both an 'invisible force' and a 'place of critical resistance'. Following on Derrida (2004), our interest in this chapter is in his enunciation of a university without condition, which holds the promise of an '*unconditional* freedom to question and to assert, or even the right to say publicly all that is required by research, knowledge, and thought concerning the *truth*' (Derrida, 2004: 11).

In Chapter 7, we bring into dispute the idea of an exclusively entrepreneurial university. The university's appeal to excellence and global competitiveness can be viewed almost exclusively, we would say, in terms of an instrumental efficiency. The primary task of a university – that of advancing knowledge in service of society – clearly accentuates the institution's drive to corporatise the university to perform an entrepreneurial role in the service of a public good whereby its knowledge becomes commodified. In this chapter, we examine what is wrong with universities in adopting an exclusive entrepreneurial culture and suggest a way to think differently about a university. We argue against such a use of a university's knowledges, in particular the idea of producing end-oriented research.

Chapter 8 makes a strong move towards cultivating a university beyond critique. Drawing on the seminal thoughts of al-Rumi, the Muslim scholar of mysticism and truth, we firstly argue that the quest or knowledge ought to have an intrinsic function – for love of the disciplines – as one cannot revere knowledge without understanding the way in which ideas and concepts evolved through the disciplines. Secondly, we show that al-Rumi's notion of togetherness also emphasises that any philosophical understanding of disciplinary knowledge ought to be grasped in relation to other distinctive disciplines and the contributions these disciplines collectively make towards an understanding of the whole. Thirdly, a university of compassion should direct its concerns for truths towards the ethical as well as, in particular, human flourishing.

In Chapter 9 – as we conclude this book – we are increasingly sensitive that our concerns might be less directed at the external influences, which compound the complexities of a university, than they are at the internal discourses and people, who collectively come to be what a university looks like. For this reason, we are intent on finding a new use for the idea of a university – one that is responsible and responsive in both its pursuit of the truth and being open to different kinds of truth, as made manifest in diverse contexts and life-worlds. Likewise, we have given consideration to notions of the metaphysical vis-à-vis truth, democracy, citizenship, critique and the ethical, such as faith, responsibility, love, compassion and togetherness. Yet, our argument has always been to find a different use for the idea of a university, even beyond its entrepreneurial status. In our efforts to profane, what a university could or should look like beyond the metaphysical and ethical, we perhaps do not want to mis-recognise the metaphysical and ethical entirely. Rather, we want to examine a new metaphysical and ethical use of a university – one commensurate with the notion of play and playfulness as enunciated by Giorgio Agamben (2007).

Chapter 9 elucidates our argument in defence of a playful university. Such a university plays with spectres of knowledges to celebrate rituals and manipulate objects and sacred words in and about a university's life. We cannot imagine a university retaining its impetus if it does not revel in research activities in which they manoeuvre traditions, foci and assertions pertaining to a university's curriculum. What play brings to the work of university scholars is, firstly, a 'playland' in which unconstrained 'pandemonium' unfolds. Secondly, we show that when pandemonium manifests in a university, uproar, bedlam, disorder and subversion of practices emanate.

In Chapter 10, we envisage that a university should remain in perpetual play. This implies three things: firstly, the professoriate can no longer keep itself busy exclusively with producing endless encyclopaedias of knowledge on the basis of reading, writing and talking. A university of playland requires that the professoriate begin to proffer (re)interpretations, creations and articulations beyond critique. Secondly, our reconfigured idea of a university is not exclusively the one that abandons rationality and a search for truths. Instead, a university-in-becoming should adopt more credible habits of reasoning driven by de-sacredised and deconstructed truths of this or that matter. Thirdly, a playful university should be the one guided by ongoing metaphysical profanations so that pedagogies of discomfort and difference be extended by those of subversiveness and witnessing. Equally, a university of play should extend its ethical enunciations beyond a pedagogy of dignity to the one of shame. Only then might we move beyond a university of critique towards the one of profanation and play.

References

Agamben, G. 2007. *Infancy and history: On the destruction of experience.* London: Verso.

Agamben, G. 2010. *Profanations.* Second edition. J. Fort (trans.). New York, NY: Zone Books.

Barnett, R. & Bengtsen, S. (Eds.) 2018. *Thinking university: A philosophical examination of thought and higher education.* Switzerland: Springer.

Derrida, J. 2004. *Eyes of the university: Right to philosophy 2.* J. Plug (trans.). Stanford, CA: Stanford University Press.

1 The thinking university reconsidered

Introduction

About a decade ago, a senior academic in the faculty where we work had left her previous institution to join us on the grounds that her new institution – our university – provides more 'head space' for her academic work. Her claim of a lack of 'head space' is worrying, because it is questionable to understand a university as a place and space where, as aptly put by Mary Evans (2004: 2), there is 'little or no time for contemplation'. When independent and critical thoughts are no longer associated with a university, such a university becomes a distortion of the values of the academy – a situation in itself that would be 'killing thinking' and accelerating 'the death of the universities' (Evans, 2004: 3). Simply put, a university devoid of 'head space' would be the one where intellectual conversation would be absent, students disengaged and academic indulgence limited. Such a university would be the one in which thinking is rare. Of course, we can account for such a university: the university remains subjected to audits, assessment and regulation; it privileges rankings and scores; it only speaks the language of performativity and managerialism; and it dishonours genuine research – that is, as enunciated by Evans (2004: 128), the university's 'academic [head] space becomes smaller and more narrowly defined.' In this chapter, we examine, firstly, what makes a thinking university what it is and, secondly, what a university should be doing to enhance the notion of a thinking university.

The university, massification and the shrinking 'head space'

It would appear that the more the university expands its reach through increasing student numbers, the less opportunity and attention are afforded to what the university ought to be doing. While mass demand for access – or massification – is seen as key to transforming both the space and the role of the university, it is also its most challenging role. The 'logic' of massification, state Altbach, Reisberg and Rumbley (2009: iii), 'is inevitable and includes greater social mobility for a growing segment of the population, new patterns of funding higher education, increasingly diversified higher education systems in most countries, generally an overall lowering of academic standards, and other tendencies.' In this sense, as noted by Akalu (2016: 262), massification has generally improved access to higher education in many countries, benefiting groups who have traditionally been excluded from elite systems of higher education.

In line with the global trend of massification, tertiary education enrolments on the African continent, and particularly, sub-Saharan Africa, have grown faster than any other region in the world – despite remaining the lowest in the world (Akalu, 2016). In the case of Africa, explains Akalu (2016: 262), massification has occurred due to two primary reasons. The first reason is linked to the increase in enrolment in primary and secondary education, thus creating a rising demand for higher education. The second reason emanates from a growing awareness on the part of African governments of the role of higher education in relation to national economic productivity. While the idea of massification in the context of post-apartheid South Africa is assumed to imply transformation, there is disagreement, however, on whether it has redressed past inequalities. On the one hand, scholars like Mohamedbhai (2008) posit that massification is key to the democratisation of access by making higher education accessible to diverse sections of the population. On the other hand, others like Hornsby and Osman (2014) hold that massification in South Africa has shown little evidence of tackling social inequalities of access and participation. This view is supported by Marginson (2016), who contends that the data reveal persisting inequalities of access to and of success within higher education, even in high participation systems, which, in turn, raises the question of equity in the management of availability and accessibility of higher education opportunities and of other factors of inequality operating within and beyond higher education systems.

In the South Africa context, which has seen massive higher education reform, Webbstock (2016: 10) explains:

> The trend to 'massification' has spawned changes in organisational structures, the size and shape of systems, in curriculum (from particular canons of knowledge to curricula that are considered relevant and useful for economic purposes), in pedagogy (from knowledge transmission to competency-based approaches, generic skills transfer, and outcomes-based approaches), in modes

of delivery (from pure classroom-based approaches to open learning or blended approaches), in research (from shifts in valuing pure research to so-called Mode 2 or applied research) and in the relationship of institutions with external communities (from town-and-gown approaches to community engagement)

Funding shortages due to massification, according to Altbach et al. (2009: xii), have also meant that higher education systems and institutions are increasingly responsible for generating larger percentages of their own revenue. They explain that the growing emphasis on cost recovery, higher tuition and university–industry links distracts from the traditional social role and service function of higher education, which are central to contemporary society.

The strong focus on access, massification and transformation at the level of students, explain Ballim and Scott (2016: 71), has meant a neglect of academic needs and the institutional culture of higher education institutions (HEIs). To Ballim and Scott (2016: 71–72), the lack of decisive pronouncement on academic matters has had the effect that the fabric of institutions – that is, human and social issues and resources – is less of a priority and should be left unchanged, or at least be deferred. The era of massification, explain Altbach et al. (2009: 17), has meant that students from a spectrum of socioeconomic backgrounds with a range of intellectual abilities now participate in higher education, thereby complicating the tasks of teaching and curriculum development. In the faculty where we are based, deliberations about the state of the university and what the university ought to be doing are often reduced to preferential conversations about curriculum redesign and pedagogical practices that will best attract and accommodate larger student bodies. Amidst ongoing debates on student numbers and student revenue, scant attention is paid to the broader concerns, which address both the intellectual and moral contributions of the faculty.

When Evans (2004: 2) argues that academics have 'little or no time for contemplation, pastoral or otherwise', she is not criticising the university's fixation with massification only. With increasing shifts towards massification comes the predominance of corporatisation and corporate discourse, which, in turn, brings into tension the idea of how knowledge is shaped and to what end. Giroux (2003: 188), for instance, asserts:

> [K]nowledge as capital in the corporate model is privileged as a form of investment in the economy, but appears to have little value when linked to the power of self-definition, social responsibility, or the capacities of individuals to expand the scope of freedom, justice, and the operations of democracy.

To Giroux (2003), the foundational impetus of a university cannot be disjointed from the imperatives of its society. If academics do not have the necessary 'head space' to engage critically with their own arguments, or if they do not have time to contemplate on the type of knowledge on offer to students, then the values of a society are at risk. To Giroux and Searls Giroux (2004: 38), the 'head space' of the university lives in what they describe as an 'agora' – a gathering or communal space, which brings together academic scholarship and civic capacities, participation and public commitment.

The corporatist discourse looms large, for example, in the recent redesign and re-curriculation of our honours programme – where the only concern is seemingly to attract higher student numbers. In support of seeing more feet passing through the proverbial doors of higher education, pedagogy has had to succumb to modes of blended learning. No doubt, blended learning has its place and necessity, especially in contexts of far-to-reach universities, but blended learning in our context has translated into a particular mass production of students and degrees, with very little concern for quality or thought.

While honours classes before constituted up to 20 students, at most (so that there is ample room for student engagement and deliberation) blended learning secures up to 50 students per module currently. High student numbers at the honours level not only discard notions of meaningful pedagogical encounters but also bring into disrepute the academic discernment of such a qualification. As enunciated by Evans (2004: 128), '[t]he paradox of contemporary universities is therefore that as the world becomes larger, the academic [head] space becomes smaller and more narrowly defined'. In our context, a number of academics have raised alarm about the academic quality of students being accepted onto the honours programme and, in turn, their own quality and standards in meeting the needs of these students. As the numbers increase, so too does the assessment and management of these students, leaving academics with little to no time for thinking or, as Evans (2004: 27) describes it, 'battery-farming for the mind', as the role of the university is reduced to meeting the needs of the market economy. Recognising what we know about the assessment-driven structure of our particular honours programme, questions have to be asked not only about the quality of education but also whether education has taken place at all. Again, Evans (2004: x) rightly observes that '[i]ncreasingly, students are being asked to pay the cost of the regulation of higher education, rather than education itself.' She argues that the 'various regulatory practices encourage mutual surveillance and informal discipline; what is never achieved through these practices is innovation, creativity or intellectual engagement' (Evans, 2004: 63).

There are many complexities that emanate from the paths of massification, which is evident in our faculty and in our university. Of primary concern is the realisation that the work of academics is de-intellectualised into blended learning frames and frameworks of measurable outcomes, with endless energy being expended on remote students, who have no need to come near the space of the university, let alone its libraries. Linked to this concern is the matter of the professoriate. On the one hand, the demands brought on through massification have led to an exponential decline of the average qualification for academics in many countries – with many teachers in developing countries having only a bachelor's degree (Altbach et al., 2009). Altbach et al. (2009: 92) report that in China, the world's largest academic system, only 9% of the academic profession has doctorates (as opposed to 70% in the top research universities); 35% of Indian academics have doctoral qualifications; in most developing countries, only academic staff at the most prestigious universities hold a doctoral degree – usually under 10% of the total. On the other hand, the proliferation of 'contract' professoriate appointments, explain Altbach et al. (2009: 91), not only undermines the promise of a university career but has also led to a differentiated and segmented academic profession. To be the most effective, they continue, professors need to be truly engaged in teaching and research. A significant proportion of profession members must have full-time academic appointments and devote attention exclusively to academic responsibilities and to the universities and colleges that employ them (Altbach et al., 2009: 91).

Instead, the full-time professoriate is in retreat, as 'contract' academics run between teaching jobs and other professions. A similar situation is encountered in private universities, where, according to Stromquist et al. (2007: 115), professors are seen as actors who dispense knowledge rather than as professionals with special rights and prerogatives.

In addition to the aforementioned, there is yet another challenge that, while more than half of the professoriate in much of the world is getting close to retirement, too few new doctorates are being produced and there are too few incentives to induce new doctorate holders to enter the profession (Altbach, Androushchak, Kuzminov, Yudkevich & Reisburg, 2013). Unsurprisingly, the latter challenge is exacerbated in developing countries, with rapidly growing student populations, such as South Africa, where there is a deep concern that there are insufficient numbers in the existing academic and postgraduate pipelines to replace the retiring cohorts. According to Altbach et al. (2009: 297), in the South African context, the loss of academic expertise at senior levels is disconcerting for institutions for many reasons, not least because it is generally at these levels that research productivity is most intense and supervision is undertaken. They continue that contradictory pressures have led to institutions adopting a range of strategies in this regard:

> While in the early years of democracy some institutions lowered their retirement age in an effort to accelerate the transformation of the demography of the academic staff body, more recently, given the effects of the loss of senior academic expertise, some have reverted to a higher retirement age.
> (Altbach et al., 2009: 297)

The point is that when the university lacks critical thought, judgement, dialogue and debate, the 'possibility and a culture of openness, debate, and engagement ... are now at risk in the latest and most dangerous attack on higher education' (Giroux, 2007: 182).

In sum, we have tried to provide a broad sense of the scope and types of challenges that affect the functioning of the university, and more specifically, how the growing trend of massification, informed by neoliberalist and corporatist conceptions of a university, brings into contestation the idea of a 'thinking' university.

What makes a thinking university what it is?

Inspired by Ron Barnett's (2016) book, *Understanding the university*, two important concerns emanate from our reading of this phenomenal text. Firstly, any attempt at understanding a university depends on knowing how such an institution organises its practices. Yet, being knowledgeable of the ways in which an understanding of a university guides its practices is to have some clarity of such an understanding (of a university) itself. Secondly, Barnett (2016) also accentuates that understanding a university is linked to having knowledge about its possibilities – that is, the possibilities that can ensue from a particular understanding of a university. This brings us to the first aspect of understanding a university.

Having some idea of what makes a university what it is seems to be connected to what Barnett (2016: 6) refers to as 'the twenty-first century ... antagonistic university'. In other words, one cannot talk about a university without invoking the notion of hostility or fractiousness or argumentativeness. By their nature and purpose, universities ought to be spaces of disagreement and contestation. For Barnett (2016: 5–7), a university is always subjected to discerning, rivalrous and turbulent movements, on the grounds that reason, judgement, integrity, impartiality, truth, knowledge, disinterestedness, critical dialogue, careful inquiry and cognitive authority are acts of discernment and rivalry that constitute and circumscribe a university. Simply put, a university without contestation would never be open to discernment, reason and judgement. How do university academics judge without troubling some view or another? How do academics reason without disagreement and argumentation? How are new forms of knowledge generated, or ideas re-imagined, if debate and argumentation are not advanced? Consequently, a university's connectedness to fractiousness and argumentativeness is what makes a university what it is.

Even before Barnett (2016), Jacques Derrida (2004: 153) associated the idea of a university with a kind of thinking that is always risky. To Derrida (2004), knowledge produced at a university cannot be for the sake of mere technical compliance, which does not respond to contemporary societal, political, economic, human and non-human complexities. According to Derrida (2004: 97), academics and students cannot be 'technicians of learning', and research at the university cannot be 'pledged in advance to some utilitarian purpose' (Derrida 2004: 111). In order for a university to be associated with thinking that is risky, it has to be autonomous, and it 'must be able, according to Kant, to teach freely whatever it wishes without conferring with anyone, letting itself be guided by its sole interest in truth' (Derrida, 2004: 104–105). In the first place, argues Derrida (2004: 97),

> [The university] is there *to tell the truth*, to judge, to criticise in the most rigorous sense of the term, namely to discern and decide between the true and the false; and if it is also entitled to decide between the just and the unjust, the moral and the immoral, this is so insofar as reason and freedom of judgement are implicated in it as well.

For Derrida (2004: 154), the act of thinking through taking risks is guided by freedom, reflection, provocation and hostility. A university devoid of such acts of thinking lacks academic autonomy 'to transform the modes of writing, the pedagogic scene, the procedures of academic exchange' (Derrida, 2004: 150). And, for a university to be a university, it has to render reasons that are provocative and discerning; otherwise, it would fail to create conditions for acts of risk and rivalry – a matter of enacting its role as an antagonistic university.

Moreover, an antagonistic university, following Barnett (2016: 9, our italics), remains on the move in 'an attempt to discern the possibilities that enable the university more fully to *play* its part in improving the world'. By implication, a university remains in potentiality – described by Barnett (2016: 2) as 'understood as being-possible', because a university 'has its possibilities; *and* they are infinite' (2016: 13). That the university is in a state of 'being' confirms that its business is *'always* unfinished' (2016: 62). A university, therefore, is invariably connected to imagining its own purposes anew and, in the process, opening ways to radically confront 'the dominant interests of our age' (Barnett, 2016: 9). For instance, nowadays, several challenges have emerged to sustainable human living and well-being in the forms of stem cell research, migration patterns, climate change and nuclear armaments. A university of possibilities should become one of finding 'new ways of taking responsibility' (Derrida, 2004: 148). This implies that such a university's thinking ought to be accompanied by 'a movement of suspicion' in relation to its responsibility to embark on what it does not have and what is not yet (Derrida, 2004: 155).

The clarification of the public role of the university, state Simons, Haverhals and Biesta (2007: 401), requires a diagnosis of the situation in which universities must try to position themselves. This, they explain, involves an investigation of the historical changes that have occurred in the fields of research and education, against the background of an evolving society that is generally said to become a knowledge society. Following Derrida (2004) and Barnett (2016), a thinking university makes meaning of the worlds in which it finds itself, then interrogates that meaning, so that new ways of thinking and being might emerge. A university such as this is not only in perpetual potentiality and fluidity but also necessarily averse to stagnation, torpor and apathy. A thinking university is as much attuned to the society in which it finds itself as it is detached in its criticism – meaning that the university is simultaneously responsive to the challenges and needs of its society, as it holds that society accountable. Societies, the world over, are in a continuous state of flux and transition, not only because of technological innovation but also because of conflict, wars, hunger and other forms of unspoken dystopias. The university, as the proverbial 'head space', has to extend its responsiveness to these transitions (whether positive or negative). This extension should not only be geared at fulfilling a moral purpose of responsibility but include the university holding itself accountable in relation to its epistemological, social and societal purposes. The thinking university does not only think about what it does but also think its own thinking and positioning in relation to the principles of integrity, morality, responsibility and compassion, as well as criticality and reflexivity.

Why would a university of play enhance the idea of a thinking university?

The modern university, according to Simons (2007: 440), is a hybrid institution, which houses different milieus and personae, each drawing upon his or her own intellectual technologies to understand the university and its public role. Currently, universities worldwide, and our institution is no exception, are witnessing a common set of developments that seem intent on expanding bureaucratic structures and processes, focused on administrative and support staff. This is counter-intuitive when what should be happening is the opening of spaces that would facilitate a more risky and rivalrous university. A thinking university requires and is desirous of efficiency not only in terms of research outputs but also in terms of academic rigour, as opposed to mere publications for the sake of publication. A thinking university is both mindful and sceptical of research outputs for the sake of utility and predetermined ranking systems, such as encountered in South Africa, which values researchers' self-commendations about their own research, rather than the integrity of the research itself. What the knowledge society needs, argues Simons (2007: 442),

> [I]s an optimal mobilization of useful brainpower in order to bring about economic prosperity (through research based innovation, sustainable employability), social welfare (through knowledge based regional development, increased higher education attainment), and democratic participation (through the promotion of citizenship competencies).

As aptly put by Barnett (2016: 89), there is gaming on the part of institutions 'in drawing up their research profile for national evaluation, so there is gaming in advancing their own research interests'. Another example is the doctoral thesis or dissertation. Instead of a doctoral thesis being concerned with its intellectual contribution to scholarship in a specific area, it seems as if such a thesis has become a space for demonstrating individual research skills. Often, such theses succumb to extensive literature reviews and data analyses taking up more than half of the document rather than a critical engagement with theoretical argumentation. Barnett (2016: 89) cogently sums up the non-rigorous doctoral thesis as follows:

> But there is often little in the way of a serious attempt to engage deeply, considerately and critically with large figures in the field ... Nor, and even more seriously, is there an attempt to carve out and sustain a definite thesis. Indeed, the very idea of 'thesis' as a focused argument that can be encapsulated sharply in a terse statement in an abstract, is entirely neglected ... The term 'thesis' is understood to refer simply to the large text in front of examiners: and 'weight' is understood to refer to the physical heaviness of the volume rather than its intellectual substance. In the process, criticality – the university's *raison de'être* at this level of a student's becoming – dwindles.

The above examples corroborate the omnipresence of the performative university – or what Jean-Francois Lyotard refers to as the 'mercantilization of knowledge' (Lyotard, 1984: 51). Our contention is that a university of possibilities should not abandon its task to cultivate thinking on the basis that thinking draws a university incessantly towards reason, reflection and criticality – that is, the *raison de'être* of a university. Only such a university can remain open to possibilities to enhance its status into the future vis-à-vis academic rigour, risk-taking and contested rivalry. In short, such a university would sustain its standing as an antagonistic university that remains open to fractiousness and argumentativeness. And, when a university continues to venture into the realm of the performative, the possibility is also there to reduce perhaps its current entrepreneurial orientation. Inasmuch as the entrepreneurial university seems to dominate and constrain a university's quest to remain antagonistic – fractious and argumentative – its current obsession with performative compliance seems to undermine and reduce its potential to remain open to possibilities 'for imaginative ventures, to assist communities and populations, at home and abroad, to understand themselves better and to live better lives' (Barnett, 2016: 97). It is for this reason that our argument in this book revolves around the notion of cultivating a university as a thinking one that remains open to what can still come.

Based on the aforementioned pronouncements, we are drawn to Giorgio Agamben's (2007) idea of play that offers a way to extend an understanding of a university beyond constrained thinking and debilitating actions that would stunt its openness to possibilities into the future. In his book, *Profanations*, Agamben (2007: 76) explains play as follows:

> Children, who play with whatever old thing falls into their hands, make toys out of things that also belong to the sphere of economics, war, law, and other activities that we are used to thinking of as serious. All of a sudden, a car, a firearm, or a legal contract becomes a toy. What is common to these cases and the profanation of the sacred is the passage from a *religio* that is now felt to be false or oppressive to negligence as *vera religio*. This, however, does not mean neglect (no kind of attention can compare to that of a child at play) but a new dimension of use, which children and philosophers give to humanity.

Our interest is in Agamben's (2007) explication of play in relation to what it means to profane. 'For to profane means not simply to abolish and erase separations but to learn to put them to a new use, to play with them ... in order to transform them into pure means' (Agamben, 2007: 87). Three aspects emanate from the aforementioned understanding of profanation. Firstly, creating a 'new use' for something implies 'deactivating an old use' of that something and thus rendering the use of it 'inoperative' (Agamben, 2007: 86). For instance, the idea of an entrepreneurial and/or performative university should be challenged and considered anew. Secondly, when a university sets out to play, it does so by reinventing the purpose of its energies. For instance, if a university were to sustain its antagonism and by implication its criticality, reason and reflection, play would open up the possibility for dissent. Elsewhere, we argue, 'dissent enhances the possibility for educational encounters to be controversial and informative, rather than just collapsing into moments of agreement without rupturing one another's intellectual perspectives' (Davids & Waghid, 2018: 148). And, considering that play gives rise to an enactment of dissent, the possibility is always there for a university in becoming open in the sense that dissent offers more spaces for a university to align itself to provocation and suspicion as such a university would be urged by the practice of dissent to do so (Davids & Waghid, 2018: 149). Put differently, dissent offers a gateway to renewed thinking and understanding so that the possibility is always there for a university to look at things as if they could be otherwise. Thirdly, to embark on play is tantamount to a political task of resistance (Agamben, 2007: 77). Such an understanding of play, that is, one that strives to uphold political resistance against acts of despair and societal destruction, seems to resonate with an idea of decoloniality that is gaining currency in African universities today. Consequently, in Chapter 8, we shall show how decoloniality – as an act of profanation – offers hope and possibilities for the future of the African university.

Summary

We commenced this chapter by offering an account of the challenges and limitations imposed upon the university through an increasing and skewed focus on massification. We paid attention to the outcome of curriculum redesign, which is geared towards reaching high numbers of students and is facilitated through regulated assessment practices, rather than the academic project and the advancement of a knowledge society. Accompanying this discussion, we focused on the precarious positioning of the professoriate – not only in terms of increasingly insecure employment agreements but also in terms of academic calibre and proficiency. Against a backdrop of the increasing influence of corporatisation and managerialism, we showed why and how the university is at risk in terms of its own knowledge production, contribution and societal standing. In turning to the seminal ideas of Derrida (2004) and Barnett (2016), we provided some offering of what might be understood by the conception of a 'thinking' university. In this regard, we looked at both the epistemological and moral imperatives of the university in relation to itself and the societies in which it finds itself. We raised questions about the university's capacity for autonomy, responsibility, criticality and finally, following Agamben (2007), the university's inclination to play, so that its energies and attention might be reinvented.

References

Agamben, G. 2007. *Profanations*. J. Fort (trans.). London: Zone Books.
Akalu, G.A. 2016. Higher education 'massification' and challenges to the professoriate: Do academics' conceptions of quality matter? *Quality in Higher Education*, 22(3): 260–276.
Altbach, P.G., Androushchak, G., Kuzminov, Y., Yudkevich, M. & Reisburg, L. (Eds.). 2013. *The global future of higher education and the academic profession: The BRICS and the United States*. New York, NY: Palgrave Macmillan.
Altbach, P.G., Reisberg, L. & Rumbley, L.E. 2009. *Trends in global higher education: Tracking an academic revolution*. A report prepared for the UNESCO 2009 World Conference on Higher Education. Paris: UNESCO.

Ballim, Y. & Scott, I. 2016. *'Regulation' in South African higher education reviewed: Two decades of democracy.* Pretoria: Council on Higher Education.
Barnett, R. 2016. *Understanding the university: Institution, idea, possibilities.* London: Routledge.
Davids, N. & Waghid, Y. 2018. *Tolerance and dissent within education.* New York, NY: Palgrave Macmillan.
Derrida, J. 2004. *Eyes of the university: Right to philosophy 2.* J. Plug (trans.). Stanford, CA: Stanford University Press.
Evans, M. 2004. *Killing thinking: The death of the universities.* London: Continuum.
Giroux, H.A. 2003. Selling out higher education. *Policy Futures in Education*, 1(1): 179–200.
Giroux, H.A. 2007. *The university in chains.* Boulder, CO: Paradigm.
Giroux, H.A. & Searls Giroux, S. 2004. *Race, youth, and the crisis of democracy in the post-civil rights era: Take back higher education.* New York, NY: Palgrave Macmillan.
Hornsby, D.J. & Osman, R. 2014. Massification in higher education: Large classes and student learning. *Higher Education*, 67(6): 711–719.
Lyotard, J.F. 1984. *The postmodern condition: A report on knowledge.* Manchester: University of Manchester Press.
Marginson, S. 2016. The worldwide trend to high participation higher education: Dynamics of social stratification in inclusive systems. *Higher Education*, 72(4): 413–434.
Mohamedbhai, G. 2008. *The effects of massification on higher education in Africa.* Accra: Association of African Universities.
Simons, M. 2007. The 'Renaissance of the University' in the European knowledge society: An exploration of principled and governmental approaches. *Studies in Philosophy and Education*, 26: 433–447.
Simons, M., Haverhals, B. & Biesta, G. 2007. Introduction: The university revisited. *Studies in Philosophy and Education*, 26: 395–404.
Stromquist, N.P., Gil-Antón, M., Colatrella, C., Reitumetse, O.M., Smolentseva, A. & Balbachevsky, E. 2007. The contemporary professoriate: Towards a diversified or segmented profession? *Higher Education Quarterly*, 61(2): 114–135.
Webbstock, D. 2016. Overview. In *South African higher education reviewed: Two decades of democracy.* Pretoria: Council on Higher Education, 5–62.

2 On searching for truth and the justification for telling the truth

Introduction

In the previous chapter, we provided some insights into the types of challenges and barriers that might restrain the university from fulfilling its responsibility as an institution of thinking. In this chapter, we extend the idea of a thinking university into the one that acts in relation to truth. Specifically, we are interested in the university, which not only searches for truth but also 'tells the truth' – that is to act with reasonable justification. Likewise, we are interested in exploring the argument that in being both responsible and responsive, the university ought to be focused on nurturing and guiding students who are best equipped to address their own truths and those of others. To search for truth is to ask questions – questions that might not necessarily yield comfortable answers, which, in turn, makes the search all the more pertinent. Here, we are reminded of the eighteenth-century German philosopher Gotthold Lessing (1979 [1778]), who pronounced:

> The true value of a man [and woman] is not determined by his [her] possession, supposed or real, of Truth, but rather by his [her] sincere exertion to get to the Truth. It is not possession of the Truth, but rather the pursuit of Truth …

Knowledge and truth

The university is geared at imparting knowledge – that is, students pursue this or that degree or programme so that they might *know*. Generally, students are exposed to two predominant forms of knowledge: propositional (knowledge *that*) and procedural (knowledge *how*). Accordingly, students may come to know that having a university education is helpful in establishing a career, or they may learn how to construct a bridge. In both these examples, knowledge, as Carr (2003: 132) explains, involves an initiation into a pre-existing set of ideas or norms. Likewise, Pring (2004: 221) asserts that knowledge is not a description of a psychological state of mind; knowledge 'depends on a publicly agreed framework of justification, refutation and verification'. Knowledge, therefore, is informed by some sort of agreement or consensus – that is, others have had to agree that a university education is helpful in establishing a career. To support the agreement, there would have to be some sort of evidence or justification, such as records of individuals who established careers because of having a university education. Having the evidence to support the agreement will lead to greater consensus – leading, in this instance, to more people pursuing a university education in the hope of similarly establishing a career.

But, of course, the propositional knowledge that having a university education is helpful in establishing a career might not be true for all individuals, and might not be true as a knowledge statement. One might find that a number of individuals, who have a university education, in fact, have not been able to establish a career. Similarly, there might be a number of people, who have indeed established a career, but without a university education. The same argument can be made in terms of the claim that an individual knows how to build a bridge. Knowing *how* to do something will not necessarily equate to successfully completing the building of the bridge. But knowledge is one way of ascertaining, whether something is true. If we know *that* an individual needs a university education in order to establish a career, then we can check or verify that. If we know *how* to build a bridge, then we can get to build a bridge – step by step – and check as we go along that the bridge is being built, based on a particular plan. And yet, inasmuch as knowledge provides us with one way of seeing or getting to the truth, how we understand truth is inextricably connected to how we see the world. We might, for instance, live in a world where a university education is neither a feasible option nor desirable in order to establish a career. We might also live in a world where the only bridge has been built by someone who did not know *how* to build a bridge before starting, but built by trial and error. Taking another example, there are many musicians – including Eric Clapton, Elvis Presley and Jimi Hendrix – who did not know *how* to read music, but who made the most amazing music.

The world, states Merleau-Ponty (2002), is a field for and of perception; hence, the world is assigned meaning through human consciousness and imagination. What we know, how we come to know and what we understand to be our truth are all influenced by how we assign meaning to the world and how we experience it. While some of us, for example, might perceive and experience the world as somewhat fatalistic, others might not. But whatever perceptions we have will play a role in how we engage with certain forms of knowledge. As individuals, we think we know what the senses of seeing, hearing or tasting are because, as Merleau-Ponty (2002: 5) explains, perception has long provided us with objects that are coloured or which emit sounds. Taste, as an example of a sense, has, according to Gadamer (1989: 32), no knowledge of reasons – '[i]f taste registers a negative reaction to something, it is not able to say why. But it experiences it with the greatest certainty.' When we taste, hear sounds or look at objects, we transpose such objects into consciousness and, according to Merleau-Ponty (2002: 5), 'we make perception out of things perceived.' Because we are caught up in a world of perception, we cannot extricate ourselves from it in order to achieve consciousness of the world (Merleau-Ponty, 2002: 5). It is, says Gadamer (1989: 124), 'the truth of our own world – the religious and moral world in which we live – that is presented before us and in which we recognize ourselves'. Gadamer (1989: xxiii) explains:

> A reflection on what truth is in the human sciences must not try to reflect itself out of the tradition whose binding force it has recognized. Hence in its own work it must endeavor to acquire as much historical self-transparency as possible. In its concern to understand the universe of understanding better than seems possible under the modern scientific notion of cognition, it has to try to establish a new relation to the concepts which it uses. It must be aware of the fact that its own understanding and interpretation are not constructions based on principles, but the furthering of an event that goes far back.

What we know and why we know it is connected to what we consider to be truth. This means that what we deem to be truth might not be the case for someone else. Even where two people participate in or experience a similar scenario, how they make meaning of it, and how they arrive at their respective truths, might not be the same. At times, truth can therefore be a subjective endeavour. Truth, contends Gadamer (1989), cannot merely and only be explained by scientific criteria or method, or by an inquiry. To him, truth transcends the limits of methodological reasoning; truth is an experience or an event in which we engage and through which we possibly change – since '[t]he truth of experience always implies an orientation toward new experience' (Gadamer 1989: 355). Following Gadamer (1989), what gives us experience as individuals, is not that we have indeed experienced this or that, but that we are open to new experiences. A person, who is open, is particularly well equipped to have new experiences and to learn from them. Likewise, as we continue this chapter, the university, which is open-minded in relation to diverse and divergent perspectives, is able to provide students with experiences that will further open themselves to their own truths and the truths of others. By engaging with our own truths, states Gadamer (1989: 299), we are 'able to experience the other's claim to truth and make it possible for him [her] to have full play himself [herself]'. In the discussion, we look at why a university ought to tell the truth, and why it ought to position itself in relation to pursuing the truth if it is to cultivate spaces of and for openness, so that new thinking might emerge.

A university ought to tell the truth

Drawing on the seminal thoughts of Jacques Derrida (2004), the task of a university should be in service of truth. In his words,

> The university is there to tell the truth, to judge, to criticize in the most rigorous sense of the term, namely to discern and decide between just and unjust, the moral and the immoral, this is so insofar as reason and freedom of judgment are implicated in it as well.
> (Derrida, 2004: 97)

The point about a Derridian understanding of telling the truth seems to be connected to at least three aspects. Firstly, a university is required to offer intransigent resistance to any abuse of power on the basis of rigorous judgements, criticisms and discernments – a matter of exercising a 'power-to-think-and-judge, a power-to-say' (Derrida, 2004: 97). The idea of power being embedded in truth is also articulated by Foucault (1977: 129), who asserts, 'truth isn't outside power, or deprived of power'; rather, truth 'is produced by virtue of multiple constraints [a]nd it induces regulated effects of power'. In other words, each society has its own 'regime of truth' and its 'general politics of truth' (Foucault, 1977: 129–130) – that is, the types of discourse and knowledge, which it both accepts and establishes as true. To Foucault (1991: 75), a resistance to power is about 'detaching the power of truth from the forms of hegemony, social, economic, and cultural, within which it operates at the present time'. As discussed in the previous chapter, the context of a reliance on state funding, on the one side, and corporations, on the other, creates intricate complexities and challenges for the university.

Giroux (180) argues that, within the prevailing discourse of neo-liberalism that has taken hold of the public imagination, 'there is no vocabulary for political or social transformation, critical education, democratically inspired visions, or critical notions of social agency to expand the meaning and purpose of democratic public life and its connection to higher education.' Yet, if the university is to think and speak for itself, then it cannot be constrained by versions of truth, and hence, versions of power.

Secondly, a university must be able to exercise its reason and freedom of judgement 'to teach freely whatever it wishes without conferring with anyone, letting itself be guided by its sole interest in the truth' (Derrida, 2004: 104). For, without the freedom to exercise its judgements, a university would be subjected to censorship, which, in turn, would not allow truth to become manifest. The point is, judging an event, for instance, depends on both one's exercise of thinking through a matter such as weighing up views on the matter, and on imagining other possible points of view (Davids & Waghid, 2017). Judging, unlike thinking (which requires autonomy and independence), requires 'worldliness, an interest in one's fellow human beings, and the capacity to appreciate the standpoint of others without projection, idealization, and distortion' (Benhabib, 2003: 191). Here, we think of increasing patterns of 'disinvitation', whereby academics or other speakers are initially invited to speak at the university, only to be disinvited as an appeasement to protests. It is a freedom to exercise judgements that is a condition of a university's autonomy where such an autonomy, in turn, is what Derrida (2004: 105) refers to the unconditioned activity of philosophy itself which controls an understanding of *universitas* and its faculties in matters arising from truth – that is, philosophy is the very soul of the university. 'Disinvitation' undermines the very idea of human engagement and deliberation. This is because the act of 'disinviting' an individual, for whatever reason, is in itself an abandonment of freedom and speech. 'Disinvitation' not only stifles any opportunity for engagement with difference and/or controversy but implies that academic freedom is the domain and preserve of those who are in agreement (Davids & Waghid, 2019).

Thirdly, for Derrida (2004: 198), a university intent on telling the truth uses the 'return of the philosophical' as a procedure to reconfigure ethico-juridical problems. In other words, using philosophy to produce, propagate and strengthen moral principles would enable a university to decide between just and unjust (Derrida, 2004: 181). It is a philosophical treatment of global cataclysms that enhance the self-destruction of humanity, such as phenomena of totalitarianism, physical and psychological torture, organ transplants, genetic manipulation and so on, which confronts the world today, which opens the possibility for 'a new reconfiguration of *ethico-juridical* problems' (Derrida, 2004: 198). This brings us to a discussion of how a university could use its capacity to tell the truth to tackle contentious concepts and practices in the world today – by doing the unexpected and the not-taken-for-granted.

Philosophy as deconstruction

Derrida (1995: 54), of course, has always been sceptical about defining what deconstruction is, although he has stated that deconstruction always aims 'at the trust confided in the critical, critico-theoretical agency, that is, the deciding agency'. Deconstruction, Derrida (1991: 275) adamantly maintains, is 'nothing'; deconstruction 'is not a method and cannot be transformed into one. ... It must also be made clear that deconstruction is not even an act or an operation' (1991: 273); deconstruction 'loses nothing from admitting that it is impossible (1991: 272); deconstruction 'doesn't consist in a set of theorems, axioms, tools, rules, techniques, methods ... there is no deconstruction, deconstruction has no specific object' (1996: 218). For us, the explanation that deconstruction, *'takes place,* it is an *event* that does not await the deliberation, consciousness, or organization of a subject' (Derrida, 1991: 274), is especially important, as we consider and reconsider what a thinking university is. Notably, the event, process or deconstruction does not come from the reader of a text, or a critique of the university (as is the concern of this text). The deconstructive process, explains Norris (1987: 19), is already there (in the university); it is the tension between what it (the text or university) 'manifestly *means to say* and what it is nonetheless *constrained to mean*'. We see this quite clearly in the increasing debates surrounding notions of academic freedom – those whose truth should be told, and those whose truth should not be allowed to be heard. Even as the university confirms its commitment to freedom of expression, its shadows impose constraint and restriction.

The recent series of #FeesMustFall campaigns, which paralysed a number of universities in South Africa (and has yet again awakened at the time of writing), provides a good, albeit disturbing example of what can happen when students (who already come from a marginalised history) are told that their voices are not worth being heard. On the one hand, the university positions itself as a democratic space of engagement and deliberation – waiting to respond to the needs of students. On the other hand, the proverbial doors of learning are shut with resounding thunder as soon as the same students dare to call the university out on both its responsibility and responsiveness. What most universities, in this case, claim is that their truth is the only truth, and in so doing, place themselves at risk in terms of what it 'manifestly *means to say*' (Norris, 1987: 19).

In searching for truth, the university is able to make the impossible possible, which not only brings into action ideas of thinking anew but reconfirms the idea of the university being in potentiality. A philosophy of deconstruction brings to a university both a language and an action to delimit constructions of truth, the centre and, hence, power. To Derrida (1984), there can be neither a centre nor an absolute, since both are constitutive of structures of power, or Foucault's (1977) 'regimes of truth'. One of the key enactments of truth – as in being true to oneself – resides in the act of forgiveness, a matter of doing the impossible in relation to another – as maintained by Arendt (1958). According to Arendt (1958: 241), when one forgives, one acts anew and unexpectedly by acting anew, by putting an end to something that without interference could go on endlessly. It is not just a matter of forgiving a past act of injustice, but also a commitment to ensuring that the past injustice will not happen again. Caputo (1996: 29) explains that Derrida's (1984) deconstruction means to consider that which is not immediately clear or present, that which is otherwise, and out of the ordinary. Caputo (1996: 29) continues,

> [The point of deconstruction] is to keep the cut of circumcision open, for circumcision is otherwise and ordinarily a mark of exclusionary membership in a community. Deconstruction traces the cut that serves us from the Truth of an Assured Destination, that keeps us "destinerrant". Deconstruction is impassioned by the cut, for that is the condition of keeping the future open, of letting the unforeseeable and unanticipatable come, of letting events happen that the horizons of the community cannot accommodate or imagine.'

By doing so, the unimaginable and the unforeseen become possible.

In dialogue with Jacques Derrida and Jürgen Habermas, Giovanna Borradori (2003) uses Derrida's (1991; 1996) understanding of deconstruction to show how philosophical analysis can be used to make certain pronouncements on forgiveness considered 'crucial both theoretically and practically to questions surrounding war crimes, genocide and terrorism' (Borradori, 2003: 139). In her words,

> Deconstruction first sets out to *identify the conceptual construction* of a given theoretical field, whether it is religion, metaphysics, or

ethical and political theory, which usually makes use of one or more irreducible pairs. Second it *highlights the hierarchical ordering* of the pairs. Third, it inverts or *subverts their ordering* by showing that the terms placed at the bottom – material, particular, temporal, and female, in this example – could with justification be moved to the top – in place of the spiritual, universal, eternal and male ... the fourth and final move is *to produce a third term* for each oppositional pair, which complicates the original load-bearing structure beyond recognition.

(Borradori, 2003: 138)

In relation to the term 'forgiveness', Derrida firstly defines its conceptual construction as 'the impossible task of forgiving the unforgivable' (2001, cited in Borradori, 2003: 140). Secondly, Derrida juxtaposes tolerance and hospitality and considers hospitality as more tenable (hierarchically ordered) than tolerance in the exercise of forgiveness. In this way, Derrida inverts hospitality and tolerance in the sense that he links forgiveness to 'the possibility of expiation [which] ... quickly leads him to expose several pairs of opposites: finite and infinite, immanent and transcendent, temporal and eternal, reparable and irreparable, expiable and inexpiable, possible and impossible' (Borradori, 2003: 142). Derrida subsequently subverts forgiveness by bestowing it to 'expiable and reparable cases ... [to] become the ground for salvation, reconciliation, redemption and atonement' (Borradori, 2003: 142). Borradori proceeds with his deconstruction of forgiveness by confounding the concept with that act, which is unforgivable:

> Derrida believes that what can be authentically forgiven is in fact only the unforgivable, whether we are talking about the act of whoever is guilty or the guilty agent herself. Forgiveness, for him, forgives both the evil intention (who) and the evil action (what) for exactly what they are: evil. And this is an evil that, insofar it is unredeemable, can repeat itself in the future.
>
> (Borradori, 2003: 143)

By implication, using deconstruction, it seems as if forgiveness 'belongs to the realm of the incalculable, the immeasurable, and maybe even the impossible ... [as] in principle, it is impossible or at least inconceivable to forgive the unforgivable' (Borradori, 2003: 142). Of course, for Derrida, unconditional forgiveness belongs to 'madness' as it arrives in the strong sense in the form of something unexpected, surprising, upsetting the ordinary understanding of the concept to assert, '[w]ithout the experience of unconditional forgiveness there would be no forgiveness at all' (Derrida, 2001, cited in Borradori, 2003: 144). What follows from the aforementioned argument is that deconstruction as a way of telling the truth is an example of how a university can or even should exercise its thinking. Next, we examine how deconstruction affects higher education.

Deconstruction and education

Gert Biesta (2009) draws our attention to the 'openness towards the other' of deconstruction (Derrida, 1984: 124, cited in Biesta, 2009). If education were to be considered an encounter between one and the other, such one and the other would always be open towards that which is unforeseeable and incoming (Caputo, 1997: 32). In other words, one and the other would open up to one another in an attempt to bring into the open that which might not be possible. According to Biesta (2009: 30),

> Deconstruction reveals that every inside has a constitutive outside that is not merely external but in a sense always inhabits the inside ... What gives deconstruction its motive and drive is precisely its concern for – or, to be more precise, its wish to do justice to – what is excluded.

Our interest is in the concern of deconstruction with the other as an act of justice. As aptly put by Biesta (2009: 31),

> If justice [and by implication, deconstruction] is a concern for the other as other ... justice is ... an experience of the impossible ... where the impossible is *not* that which is not possible, but that which cannot be foreseen as a possibility.'

And, if education is an encounter between one and the other, and such an encounter is guided by justice, then deconstruction (as justice) makes education that which remains 'on the outlook for the impossible invention of the other' (Biesta, 2009: 35). Put more succinctly, education, guided by deconstruction, invariably prepares university teachers and students for the 'incalculable' (Biesta, 2009: 35). Thus, when teachers respond to students in a just manner, 'something incalculable comes on the scene [which] gives deconstruction its movement' (Derrida, 1997: 18).

Based on the aforementioned understanding of deconstruction, justice and education, it follows that if the task of a university is to tell the truth, then such a university is concerned to be responsive to others within their otherness. This implies that the university would be open to that which does not seem possible, the incalculable. A university guided by justice through telling the truth keeps the surprise of the other open – what Biesta (2009: 35) refers to as 'to be on the outlook for the impossible invention of the other'. In turn, the university, which is intent upon searching for the truth, remains open to the unforeseen and unpredictable, is prepared to change and is prepared to acknowledge plurality of thinking, being, believing and knowing – so that nothing is determined as absolute or closed.

In conclusion, the idea of deconstruction in education, coupled with the idea of the university as a space of deconstruction, implies that the university cannot lay claim to an authoritative or hierarchical truth. In other words, if the university is to remain open to the new and the unexpected, then its own sense of authority is always in potentiality and in flux. As a potential site and medium for and of deconstruction, the university has to be looking inward, towards itself in order to be open to that which is not immediately evident. In this way, a thinking university is always open and exposed, and as such, the very vulnerability, which accompanies this openness, becomes its greatest strength.

Summary

We started this chapter by touching on the inter-connectivity between knowledge and truth, and showed how truth is always shaped by pre-existing frameworks, and perceptions of how we see and experience the world. Drawing on the ideas of Derrida – in relation to truth and deconstruction – we argued that the university should not only be telling the truth but be open in its pursuit of the truths of others. By focusing on Derrida's deconstruction, we showed how the university as a place and space is already within a deconstructive process or event – that is, deconstruction is not something which comes from the outside, and happens *to* the university, but rather deconstruction is already present in what the university means to say and do, and does not say and do.

References

Arendt, H. 1958. *The human condition*. Chicago, IL: Chicago University Press.
Benhabib, S. 2003. *The reluctant modernism of Hannah Arendt*. New York, NY: Rowman & Littlefield Publishers Inc.
Biesta, G. 2009. Deconstruction, justice, and the vocation of education. In M.A. Peters & G. Biesta (eds.). *Derrida, deconstruction, and the politics of pedagogy*. New York, NY: Peter Lang, 15–38.

Borradori, G. 2003. *Philosophy in a time of terror: Dialogues with Jürgen Habermas and Jacques Derrida.* Chicago, IL: The University of Chicago Press.

Caputo, J.D. 1996. Community without truth: Derrida and the impossible community. *Research in Phenomenology,* 26: 25–37.

Caputo, J.D. (Ed.). 1997. *Deconstruction in a nutshell: A conversation with Jacques Derrida.* New York, NY: Fordham University Press.

Carr, D. 2003. *Making sense of education: An introduction to the philosophy and theory of education and teaching.* London: Routledge Falmer.

Davids, N. & Waghid, Y. 2017. *Tolerance and dissent within education: On cultivating debate and understanding.* New York, NY: Palgrave Macmillan.

Davids, N. & Waghid, Y. 2019. *Free speech, universities and pedagogical encounters: Reconfiguring democratic education.* Lanham, MD: Rowman & Littlefield.

Derrida, J. 1984. Deconstruction and the other: An interview with Jacques Derrida. In R. Kearney (ed.). *Dialogues with contemporary continental thinkers: The phenomenological heritage.* Manchester: Manchester University Press, 120–126.

Derrida, J. 1991. Letter to a Japanese friend. In P. Kamuf (ed.). *A Derrida reader.* New York, NY: Harvester, 270–276.

Derrida, J. 1995. *Points ... interviews, 1974–1994.* Stanford, CA: Stanford University Press.

Derrida, J. 1996. 'As if I were dead': An interview with Jacques Derrida. In J. Brannigan, R. Robbins & J. Wolfreys (eds.). *Applying: To Derrida.* London: Macmillan, 212–227.

Derrida, J. 1997. The Villanova roundtable: A conversation with Jacques Derrida. In J.D. Caputo (ed.). *Deconstruction in a nutshell: A conversation with Jacques Derrida.* New York, NY: Fordham University Press, 31–47.

Derrida, J. 2004. *Eyes of the university: Right to philosophy 2.* J. Plug (trans.). Stanford, CA: Stanford University Press.

Foucault, M. 1977. *Discipline and punish: The birth of the prison.* A. Sheridan (trans.). London: Penguin Books.

Foucault, M. 1991. Governmentality. In Burchell, G., Gordon, C. & Miller, P. (eds.), *The Foucault effect: Studies in governmentality.* Chicago: University of Chicago Press, 87–104.

Gadamer, H.G. 1989. *Truth and method.* J. Weinsheimer & D.G. Marshall (trans.). New York, NY: Crossroad.

Giroux, H.A. 2003. Selling out higher education. *Policy Futures in Education,* 1(1): 179–200.

Lessing, G.E. 1979 [1778]. *Anti-Goetze: Eine Duplik.* S. Horton (trans.), H. Göpfert (ed.). *Werke,* 8: 32–33.

Merleau-Ponty, M. 2002. *Phenomenology of perception.* London: Routledge.

Norris, C. 1987. *Derrida.* London: Fontana.

Pring, R. 2004. *Philosophy of education: Aims, theory, common sense and research.* London: Continuum.

3 Student alienation and the democratic mission of a university re-examined

Introduction

We introduced this book with a connectedness to profanation to consider and give a new use to the idea of a university – that is, to bring into attention the notion of a university of truth and of play. If a university is to foster openness, where divergent points of view are brought into play, then this implies being willing to listen to and engage with radical ways of thinking and being. A university, as we know, is primarily underscored by practices of teaching and learning and, hence, teachers and students. University teachers, by virtue of their respective disciplines and academic profiles, bring with them diverse sets of knowledge, skills and teaching pedagogies, as well as ideas of what ought to happen in their classrooms. In turn, students arrive with and within their own ideas and expectations of what ought to unfold in an academic environment. While teachers or academics might have a clear sense of who they are and how they fit into university spaces and norms, this is often not the case for students. Instead, increasing patterns of massification in higher education has predictably meant increasing experiences of displacement and anxiety. Students often arrive with a great sense of reticence, filtered through experiences of non-belonging and manifested through academic alienation. The concern of this chapter is, firstly, to look at common causes and experiences of alienation within a university and, secondly, to consider how the university might provide a different space of pedagogical engagement – one in which alienation is subverted. The chapter, therefore, is interested in re-examining the democratic mission of a university, and how this might radicalise relations among teachers and students in a university.

The university student and academic alienation

It is not unusual for students to experience uncertainty and insecurity as they transition from the school to a university environment. There are, of course, a myriad of reasons for the anxieties, which accompany this transition – from living away from home for the first time (as is the case for most students) to bigger classes, new found independence and a set of expectations, which are largely unknown. The transition is amplified when one takes into account particular historical, political, economic and social contexts, which cannot be divorced from the student experience. The South African context presents an example where the majority of students come from historical and generational exclusion. Since becoming a democracy in 1994, South Africa has doubled the number of students in higher education, and currently has about one million students in the system, which constitutes 20% of the 18- to 23-year-old age cohort (Case, Marshall, McKenna & Mogashana, 2018: 11). Massification of higher education, as noted by Ashwin and Case (2018: 6), is typically, but not inevitably, accompanied by increased stratification – '[s]tratification limits higher education's capacity to be an engine for social mobility because there are disparities in who has access to the most prestigious universities, which are seen to offer the highest economic and social returns.' In agreement, Tinto (2003: 2) contends that students, especially those historically excluded from higher education, are affected 'by the campus expectational climate and by their perceptions of the expectations of faculty and staff hold for their individual performance.' There is an argument, according to Case et al. (2018: 3), 'that the forms of knowledge and associated literacy practices that are valued in the academy are those of privileged groups in society, and that the university mainly serves to prop up this privilege'. In the South African context, a report tabled by the Council on Higher Education (CHE, 2013) revealed poor student throughput and low retention. Only 30% of students, registered for a three-year bachelor's degree, managed to complete their degrees within the stipulated three years, with 56% graduating within a five-year period.

Following the above, while the transition from the school to the university is not only influenced by academic demands, the measurement of student retention and degree completion, however, depends on academic performance and achievement. It is in the university classroom where students experience the highest sense of displacement and alienation – because they are not 'seen', and because of many complexities they are unable to navigate the expectations of the classroom.

Boughey and McKenna (2016: 1) refer to the 'decontextualised learner' in order to describe the ways in which students are often understood as separate from the socio-cultural world. Within this discourse, Hlengwa, McKenna and Njovane (2018: 55) explain that the student is stripped of heritage, norms, values and social practices. The success and failure of the student in higher education are understood to emerge from characteristics inherent in him or her as an individual. Unsurprisingly, notions of the 'decontextualised learner' (Boughey & McKenna, 2016) give rise to student alienation.

To Mann (2001: 8), the experience of alienation within the learning environment can be defined as 'the estrangement of the learner from what they should be engaged in, namely the subject and process of study itself'. When students experience alienation, says Mann (2005: 43), they feel unable to engage or contribute in ways that are meaningful and productive for the realisation of their own potential and learning requirements. This may include, Mann continues, the experience of feeling held back, blocked, inhibited, estranged or isolated from what it is they are learning, and the study practices and learning processes – both individual and social – that are part of their particular learning context. Consequently, argues Mann (2001: 7), it is not unusual to find learners or students adopting either a *'surface* approach to their study', characterised by a focus on rote learning, memorisation and reproduction, a lack of reflection and a preoccupation with completing the task, or a *'strategic* approach', characterised by a focus on assessment requirements and lecturer expectations, and a careful management of time and effort with the aim of achieving high grades. In the case of a 'surface approach', continues Mann (2001: 7), the student is understood to be *'passively* undertaking perceived requirements in a way that does not engage their being and desires in the subject of study, but locates the responsibility for their actions and purposes in an external other'. In a *'strategic* approach',

> [The student could] *actively* [be] undertaking perceived requirements in order to fulfil their own desires for success, but doing this in such a way that does not allow them to engage their own being and desires in relation to the subject of study itself, and which locates control for their engagement in the perceived demands and criteria for success of external others.
>
> (Mann, 2001: 7)

According to Mann (2001: 7), both approaches could be described as 'expressing an alienation from the subject and process of study itself'.

While the university might be aware of the experiences of student alienation from the classroom, and hence their own learning, the common response is corrective, rather than attempting to take into account who the student is, what he or she expects and what his or her actual experiences are. Hence, because the university persists in understanding students as 'decontextualised', it continues to want to remedy the problem of poor academic performance and achievement through remedial add-on interventions. These recommendations, explain Hlengwa et al. (2018: 157), include calls for academic support in the form of additional tutorials, supplementary instruction, online courses or enhanced orientation programmes. While such initiatives may well be beneficial to the student, Hlengwa et al. (2018: 157) argue, 'they are arguably based on the premise that both the problem and the solution rest outside of the core university structures and cultures, the curriculum content or the teaching and assessment approaches.' On the one hand, therefore, a university 'remains largely untouched while students are slotted into various initiatives to fix the lacks they have' (Hlengwa et al., 2018: 157). On the other hand, complex questions arise about how a university is conceived in relation to how it is experienced. If a number of students are alienated and disengaged from their own learning, then the university has brought into disrepute notions of inclusivity, belonging, recognition and accountability – values commonly associated with the idea of a democratic university. How then might a thinking university begin to establish an academic culture, based on student attachment and engagement with their learning, and hence a university?

Students, academic culture and belonging

Even before students have attended their first lecture or attempted their first essay, they will have begun the process of confronting and negotiating the (largely unwritten) 'rules of the game' of university life (Read, Archer & Leathwood, 2003: 261). Although the dominant discourses of knowledge, communication and practice in higher education can be seen to vary significantly geographically, politically, socially and economically, as well as between institutions, between faculties and between disciplines, Read et al. (2003) nevertheless refer to these discourses as constituting an 'academic culture'. The academic and institutional culture are influenced and shaped by how the university defines itself in relation to knowledge, research, teaching and community engagement. It is also shaped by its policies of access, teacher and student bodies. The identity of a university, according to Tierney and Lanford (2018: 1), is often not definable, 'especially since the culture of an institution is both subjective – depending on the perspectives and motivations of different individuals – and complex – moving beyond the descriptive clarity offered by organizational charts and quantitative measurements of institutional progress'. Moreover, for Tierney and Lanford (2018: 2), one's understanding of institutional culture is subject to reinterpretation as new individuals instigate change through the unique perspectives and ideas they introduce and propagate. For these reasons, the authors continue, most contemporary discussions of institutional culture proceed from the epistemological stipulation that the organisational environment of higher education is 'socially constructed' (Tierney & Lanford, 2018: 2). Hence, institutional and academic cultures, as observed by Read et al. (2003: 61), are neither uniformly accessed nor experienced. Despite massification and the significant increase in students from the working class and from ethnically diverse backgrounds attending university in the last two decades, academic culture predominantly reflects the dominant discourse of the student as white, middle class and male (Read et al., 2003).

The South African higher education landscape provides a rich kaleidoscope of deeply embedded disparities. Although there have been significant shifts in the student demographics at historically advantaged institutions, historically disadvantaged institutions have retained their historic racially and culturally defined identity. Despite student migratory patterns at historically advantaged institutions, it is hard to pinpoint any definitive shifts in the institutional and academic cultures, with the overwhelming criticism being that these institutions continue to perpetuate a culture of white privilege. Shay (2016) explains that, as recently as 2015 – with the '#FeesMustFall' and '#RhodesMustFall' campaigns – students have called for the end of domination by 'white, male, Western, capitalist, heterosexual, European worldviews' in higher education and incorporation of other South African, African and global 'perspectives, experiences [and] epistemologies' as the central tenets of the curriculum, teaching, learning and research in the country.

Despite massive reform in higher education in South Africa, which included the objective of epistemological transformation through a 'reorientation away from the apartheid knowledge system, in which curriculum was used as a tool of exclusion, to a democratic curriculum that is inclusive of all human thought' (Department of Education [DoE], 2008: 89), the curriculum has remained largely intact. By the admission of the Department of Education, transformation efforts have not 'translated into any significant shifts in the structure and content of the curriculum' (DoE, 2008: 90), and the curriculum 'is inextricably intertwined with the institutional culture and, given that the latter remains white and Eurocentric at the historically white institutions, the institutional environment is not conducive to curriculum reform' (DoE, 2008: 91).

When students fail to find a point of resonance with the university, especially in and through their own learning, it becomes highly improbable for them to claim responsibility and accountability for their own education. Finding a point of resonance or attachment provides a marker of belonging, which allows the student to come into the presence of both his or her learning and a university. Mann (2001: 45) argues that it is possible for students to counter the potential experience of alienation in the learning environment by establishing learning communities in which a sense of belonging, shared purpose, relatedness and support are fostered as a necessary first step in establishing collaborative learning. In this regard, we are drawn to Agamben's (1993) idea of community, as not only providing a shared sense of belonging but also one that is always in potentiality or a state of becoming. To Agamben (1993), a conception of community does not presuppose commonality or identity as a condition of belonging. Rather, the coming community is the one where '[whatever] singularities form a community without affirming an identity, that humans co-belong, without any representable condition of belonging' (Agamben, 1993: 86). The 'whatever' in question for Agamben (1993: 1) 'relates to singularity not in its indifference with respect to a common property (to a concept, for example: being red, being French, being Muslim), but only in its being *such as it is*'. For one, students would not be taught to share differences and commonalities as they tackle important human-affected issues in society. Rather, without affirming their identities, they are taught to address issues in society that affect them as humans who co-belong, without insisting on establishing a shared intersubjective community that should tackle the issues with a common identity (Waghid & Davids, 2013).

The idea of constituting a community of co-belonging is important not only as a counter to experiences of alienation but also as an enactment of democratic engagement, whereby students (as is the case here) might come together in their singularities and enact their potentiality. Since we have drawn on Derrida in the previous chapter, it is worth mentioning that Agamben's (1993) conception of community is decidedly different to that of Derrida – a construction which Derrida, in fact, disliked. Agamben's community is neither homogenous nor closed to the possibility of thinking anew and differently about how things can be. To him, coming together as a community does not imply any sort of exclusion, since the individual might come and leave again in any singularity. In this sense, a community which co-belongs with the common purpose of changing the way teaching and learning unfold in a university, for example, does not know any boundaries or restrictions. Most importantly, this community is not constituted on the basis of consensus or compliance, but rather, for the purposes of dissensus, so that thinking might abound. Next, we turn our attention to the idea of the university as being a space of radical thinking, engagement and deliberation.

Towards a radical democratic university

Undeniably, a university is a space where democratic moments manifest: teachers and students engage with one another; they (teachers and students) exercise their communicative freedom; and, they are exposed to one another as equals in the sense that they have equal access to a book, a text, a computer, a classroom and so on. However, the concern of this section pertains to the nature of their democratic moments. Concomitantly with the idea that a university allows spaces for democratic moments is the possibility that undemocratic encounters could arise such as when some students are excluded from pedagogical encounters, teachers being inattentive to students' learning experiences, and some teachers assuming the roles of master explicators in the sense that students are denied the right to exercise their equal intelligence. Simply put, teachers act as authoritative agents without creating conditions for students to come to speech. As a result, teachers lay claim to being the only voices of authority, and students are expected to listen passively and absorb knowledge, as opposed to engaging and deliberating actively on what is being taught and learned. When students are not invited to participate and to speak back, to question and to disagree, they become docile and unresponsive participants in their own learning. In turn, in a classroom where there are no opportunities for deliberation and debate, existing views and arguments remain uncontested, thereby stifling opportunities for new ways of thinking and considerations to come to the fore.

Implicit in the aforementioned description of an undemocratic university is an understanding that such a university ought to become more radicalised in a democratic way. In reference to the seminal thoughts of Jacques Rancière (1991, 1995, 2007), we shall now examine what a radicalised democratic university could possibly look like.

Firstly, a university ought to be a place where students and teachers speak; otherwise, they would be unfree or not emancipated (Rancière (1991: 65). When students, for example, speak, they possess the ability to come to their own speech – that is, students use their intelligence. Such a kind of university education that recognises students' right to speak or their capacity for speech provokes equality. To start from the view that all students are speaking beings is to invoke the assumption of equality in the sense that students can exercise their equal intelligence (Rancière, 1991: 46). Think about the many ways in which equality of intelligence could guide pedagogical relations among students and teachers, negotiations in meetings about university policies and university management's handling of student disruptions. The aforementioned encounters could be more democratic when those who supposedly have no power in the relationships demonstrate their equality by interrupting such encounters to make things unfold. As cogently put by Maarten Simons and Jan Masschelein (2011: 6), '[t]he capacity power of the *demos*, which is not the power of the people or its majority, [is the] the power or capacity of no matter who (or whoever).'

It is especially when those considered not as powerful as others actually demonstrate their equal intelligence by disrupting the chain of argumentation and justification that a radicalised form of democracy in human encounters manifests. It is usually the case that less eloquent persons do not always dominate democratic encounters. However, when they exercise their equality and come to speech, the possibility arises that they disrupt the encounters. The point is, when human encounters 'start from equality and allow the new generation [of university students and teachers] to be in the presence of something and to respond to that presence' (Cornelisen, 2011: 29), radicalised democratic relationships ensue. It is usually assumed by many teachers and students that the latter (students) are less powerful and hence do not possess the capacity to disrupt encounters among themselves and teachers. What a radicalised democratic relationship involves is for students to exercise their capacity to the extent that they effect such a relationship.

Secondly, in a radicalised democratic university, more time is afforded to the practice of attentiveness. Being attentive implies that university teachers start from the premise that all students are able to make sense of what is open for deliberation. And for deliberative encounters to take place, teachers require of students to be attentive 'to what is on the table and to make the experience of a new use possible at all' – as a profane university expects of them to do (Masschelein & Simons, 2011: 163). As soon as teachers start their possible engagement with students from the assumption that they (students) are not able to deliberate about matters concerning university education, then the possibility that students become attentive would be minimised or even ruled out in its entirety. In other words, students are not just left to their own devices; rather, they are summoned to engage with this or that matter, which concerns them. The possibility of attentiveness recognises students as present and not absent from deliberative encounters. Such teachers are passionate and care about students corroborated by their concern for and presence of students. In a non-radicalised university, students are often involved in participating in relation to address particular concerns. Although they (students) participate, they do not always effect change to the initiatives of the institution regarding curriculum, policy and management issues. However, when they (students) are summoned to engage, they are being attended to in the sense that they are invited to proffer judgements that can shape the course of institutional events differently. This is a consequence of them being present. By being there, they (students) legitimately proffer understandings that are taken seriously by others.

Thirdly, if a university were to have a democratic mission, such an institution becomes obliged to cultivate within its relations among teachers and students, what Carl Anders Säfström (2011: 101) refers to as a 'pedagogy of dissensus'. Of course, following Rancière (2003: 226), dissensus is not the 'opposition of interests or opinions'; rather, 'it is the production, within a determined, sensible world, of a given that is heterogenous to it'. As Biesta (2011: 37) explains, dissensus is not a quarrel, 'but is a gap in the very configuration of sensible concepts, a dissociation introduced into the correspondence between ways of being and ways of doing, seeing, and speaking'. We concur with Säfström (2011: 101) that the task of democracy in (higher) education is to go beyond the idea that there can be education without emancipation. The moment this happens, everyone will not only have the right to be heard but also be transformed into an equal speaking being on the grounds that a pedagogy of dissensus 'strives to create the conditions for the equality of relationships between everyone by asking the question – what do you think differently?' (Säfström, 2011: 102). Again, Säfström (2011: 102) explains as follows:

> The speaking being establishes herself as a legitimate speaker by taking the role of not just any speaker but by attaching herself to the conflict between pairs of society. By so doing she takes the form of a singular universal, that is, addressing a singular event, the immediate suffering of exclusion, inequality and cruelty, as an embodiment of unequal society as such ... [that] dissensus is introduced in an educational form that imitates democratic politics.

Thus, calling for a pedagogy of dissensus in university education could bring about an attentiveness to disturbances that may, in fact, radicalise democratic (higher) education. This is so because such a pedagogy would make university teachers and students attentive to the particularities of the social order within which we live that requires an emancipation of the individual self (Säfström 2011: 94).

In sum, in a radicalised democratic university, 'all sit as equals around the same table, and confronted with what lies on the table anything can happen and no-one can claim an authority to say what should be done' (Masschelein & Simons, 2011: 164). This implies that all voices are taken into account and, more importantly, that a thinking university advocates inclusivity, so that its democratic mission is not undermined through any practices of exclusion. For instance, in a radicalised democratic university, university professors do not just tell students what decisions have been taken and then students should oblige. Rather, decisions are deliberated upon as equals on the part of teachers and students with the possibility that all will be inspired to come up with things not thought of before. Divergent and conflicting viewpoints are included, so that what is cultivated is active participation through deliberation and debate.

As educators, states Giroux (1992: 9),

> [We need] to recognize the partiality of our own views in order to render them more suspect and open ended; we need to create the conditions and safe spaces that offer teachers and students the opportunity to be border crossers, learn new languages, refigure the boundaries of interdisciplinary discourse, and consistently work to make the familiar strange and the given problematic.

Clearly, relations among university teachers and students in post-apartheid South Africa would gain from such an understanding that decisions are not predetermined in advance and for students simply to abide by their implementation. As long as both students and teachers are present and included to make deliberative decisions, a radicalised democratic university would remain in becoming.

The point about bringing the idea of a radicalised democratic in conversation with a university invariably affects the human encounters among teachers and students in a different way – one perhaps not practised previously. In such a situation, all involved in university education exercise their right to speak and by implication to come to speech. By being summoned to speak their minds, the less authoritative is not only proffering views but also invited to offer judgements that can alter this or that situation pertaining to university education. That is, they would be summoned to act with equality in attending to university matters. What would be high on the agenda of all university equals would be the cultivation of a politics of dissensus where individuals and a collective could evoke understandings that will disturb the academic order of university life.

Summary

This chapter started by taking into account the challenges that students encounter as they transition from a school to a university environment. Particular attention was given to the risks of alienation, as students from diverse and pluralist backgrounds converge in one space, and particular classroom practices might add to the experiences of alienation and non-belonging of students. In response, we looked at how students might embark on establishing their own academic culture, by co-belonging within communities, with the purpose of addressing common challenges. Following on this, we considered various options and approaches, which might ensure the university space as the one where democracy manifests. In this regard, we argued for the idea of a radical democratic university – one in which both teachers and students exercise their communicative freedom, by being summoned to speak their minds.

References

Agamben, G. 1993. *The coming community: Theory out of bounds.* Volume 1. M. Hardt (trans.). Minneapolis: University of Minnesota Press.

Ashwin, P. & Case, J.M. (Eds.). 2018. *Higher education pathways: South African undergraduate education and the public good.* Cape Town: African Minds.

Biesta, G. 2011. Learner, student, speaker: Why it matters how we call those we teach. In M. Simons & J. Masschelein (eds.). *Rancière, public education and the taming of democracy.* London: Wiley-Blackwell, 31–42.

Boughey, C. & McKenna, S. 2016. Academic literacy and the decontextualized learner. *Critical Studies in Teaching and Learning,* 4(2):1–9.

Case, J.M., Marshall, D., McKenna, S. & Mogashana, D. 2018. *Going to university: The influence of higher education on the lives of young South Africans.* Higher Education Dynamics Series Volume 3. Cape Town: African Minds.

CHE (Council on Higher Education). 2013. *A proposal for undergraduate curriculum reform in South Africa: The case for a flexible curriculum structure.* Pretoria.

Cornelisen, G. 2011. The public role of teaching: To keep the door closed. In M. Simons & J. Masschelein (eds.). *Rancière, public education and the taming of democracy.* London: Wiley-Blackwell, 15–30.

DoE (Department of Education). 2008. *Report of the ministerial committee on transformation and social cohesion and the elimination of discrimination in public higher education institutions.* Pretoria.

Giroux, H.A. 1992. Educational leadership and the crisis of democratic government. *Educational Researcher*, 21(4): 4–11.

Hlengwa, A., McKenna, S. & Njovane, T. 2018. The lenses we use to research student experiences. In P. Ashwin & J.M. Case (eds.). *Higher education pathways: South African undergraduate education and the public good.* Cape Town: African Minds, 149–162.

Mann, S.J. 2001. Alternative perspectives on student learning: Alienation and engagement. *Studies in Higher Education*, 26(1): 7–19.

Mann, S.J. 2005. Alienation in the learning environment: A failure of community? *Studies in Higher Education*, 30(1): 43–55.

Masschelein, J. & Simons, M. 2011. The hatred of public schooling: The school as the mark of democracy. In M. Simons & J. Masschelein (eds.). *Rancière, public education and the taming of democracy.* London: Wiley-Blackwell, 150–165.

Rancière, J. 1991. *The ignorant schoolmaster: Five lessons in intellectual emancipation.* K. Ross (trans.). Stanford, CA: Stanford University Press.

Rancière, J. 1995. *On the shores of politics.* London: Verso.

Rancière, J. 2003. *The philosopher and his poor.* Durham, NC: Duke University Press.

Rancière, J. 2007. *Hatred of democracy.* S. Corocoran (trans.). London: Verso.

Read, B., Archer, L. & Leathwood, C. (2003) Challenging cultures? Student conceptions of 'belonging' and 'isolation' at a post-1992 university. *Studies in Higher Education*, 28(3): 261–277.

Säfström, C.A. 2011. The immigrant has not proper name. In M. Simons & J. Masschelein (eds.). *Rancière, public education and the taming of democracy.* London: Wiley-Blackwell, 93–104.

Shay, S. 2016. Decolonising the curriculum: It's time for a strategy. *The Conversation*, 13 June. Retrieved from https://theconversation.com/decolonising-the-curriculum-its-time-for-a-strategy-60598 [Accessed 15 February 2019].

Simons, M. & Masschelein, J. 2011. Introduction: Hatred of democracy … and of the public role of education? In M. Simons & J. Masschelein (eds.). *Rancière, public education and the taming of democracy.* London: Wiley-Blackwell, 1–14.

Tierney, W.G. & Lanford, M. 2018. Institutional culture in higher education. In J.C. Shin & P. Teixeira (eds.). *Encyclopedia of international higher education systems and institutions.* Dordrecht: Springer, 1–9.

Tinto, V. 2003. Promoting student retention through classroom practice. Paper presented at Enhancing Student Retention: Using International Policy and Practice. Staffordshire University, November 5–7, 2003.

Waghid, Y. & Davids, N. 2013. *Citizenship education and violence in schools: On disrupted potentialities and becoming.* Rotterdam: Sense.

4 On some of the limitations of citizenship and the thinking university

Introduction

Opening up a university to a new use invariably brings into play the idea of the public mission of a university. Extensive work has already been done in this area, most notably in and about the public responsibility of a university in the context of knowledge production (Rhoten & Calhoun, 2011). The Council on Higher Education (CHE) in South Africa has also committed itself to the cultivation of the public responsibility of a university (CHE, 2013). The idea of the public responsibility of a university mostly centres on issues of equitable redress, and the cultivation of a democratic citizenry after decades of repressive apartheid governance. Understandably, the focus on cultivating a democratic citizenry is primarily linked to enhancing economic, political and social stabilities. Hence, it is not inappropriate to think of a university in post-apartheid South Africa vis-à-vis the advocacy for a democratic citizenry. In this chapter, we firstly specifically take a close look at why and how the public responsibility of a university can be linked to enabling renewed attention on democratic citizenship. Secondly, we show how the cultivation of democratic citizenship seems to be commensurable with the idea of producing a thinking university. Thirdly, we identify some of the limitations of democratic citizenship – in particular its emphasis on patriotism – which can undermine any defensible form of a thinking university.

Public responsibility of a university and the cultivation of democratic citizenship

Craig Calhoun (2011: 6–7) reminds us that the public mission of a university is closely linked to the public character of its work: publication, innovation, judgement and debates on important public issues.

Together with the aforementioned view of the public mission of a university, he also accentuates an important point, '[i]t's not just that universities educate *citizens*, it is that in certain ways science has been one of the great models for the kind of behavior citizens need to practice for democracy …' (Calhoun, 2011: 7). Considering that the pursuit of science involves 'a free and open debate among researchers that can drive forward critical inquiry, correct errors, and ensure ideas gain support from their intellectual quality – mainly on the bases of logic and evidence …' (Calhoun, 2011: 6), this implies that cultivating democratic citizenship – an important public mission of a university – cannot be remiss of producing educated democratic citizens who are free, open and critical in their intellectual ventures of knowledge production. The latter is what Calhoun (2011: 7–8) refers to as 'the pursuit of truth' in the sense that a university shapes 'a democratic-pragmatist way of thinking about authoritative knowledge in science … [that is] a matter of making knowledge public …' – equally so, responding in a responsible manner.

In a similar fashion, Derrida (2004: 91) equates responsibility with 'a summons requiring a response'. This infers that when a university is summoned or called upon to act in response to a particular situation – whether it is climate change, food security, water scarcity or poor literacy levels – it does so by acting responsibly. When Derrida (2004: 148) describes the university as 'the responsibility of a community of thinking', he has in mind both its reason (to be) and its justification (for being). In other words, the university is as much a part of the community in which it finds itself as it stands outside of it in as far as such university needs to justify its existence through noble intents. In this sense, the university has the choice to respond or not to respond and how to respond – that is, acting with 'freedom of judgement' (Derrida, 2004: 97). By finding reason to respond or act, the university acts with justification, but by so doing, takes a risk, because the university cannot know what is yet to come (Derrida, 2004: 155). In other words, acting with justification, as well as taking risks, can lead to achieving the unexpected or the improbable.

If we relate the idea of responsibility to citizenship education, then it can be said that responsible citizenship education ought to engender understandings that students should be encouraged to take risks coupled with giving an account of their citizenship (Waghid & Davids, 2013). The recent series of student protests – commonly referred to as the #FeesMustFall and #RhodesMustFall campaigns in South Africa – raised critical and justifiable questions about the conduct of students, and how plans of protest are enacted. On the one hand, the students had legitimate and just reasons for protesting against university fees, and against what is perceived to be the prevalence of institutional colonialism at historically advantaged universities. In a context where black students continue to enjoy the lowest levels of access, and face increasing levels of attrition because of their incapacity to pay fees, the call to protest by students was a responsible response to an unjust system. On the other hand, however, their protests stood accused of wanton violence, vandalism and destruction, as students burnt and destroyed libraries and lecture theatres, and prevented other students from exercising their right to attend class or to write examinations.

What started as a legitimate form of expression and contestation against the marginalisation structures (fees and colonialism) encountered in university spaces soon deteriorated into a vitriol of uncontrolled violence, leading to the suspension of classes, disruption of examinations and the temporary closure of a number of universities. In this scenario, vital values of democratic citizenship and democratic ways of being were transgressed. While students need to be commended for taking the risk of protesting against university structures, they need to be remanded for allowing their protests to degenerate into violence. A thinking university of responsibility would need to reflect upon the student protests, and use these as an educative moment for what democracy means, and when the boundaries of democracy are over-stepped. The risk of action cannot translate into a risk of safety and well-being. The conception of responsibility for which we are arguing here is strongly connected to a moral action that is informed by a sense of fairness and justice. To Derrida (2004), justice comes in the form of responsibility to the other as difference – that every individual has a responsibility to live with the other and to treat the otherness of the other justly. It also means that, in order to live responsibly, we have to live with others and be mindful of how we treat each other. In not acting responsibly, one does not enact one's humanity in relation to the other and, by so doing, fails to recognise that one's humanity is so because of a relational co-belonging (Waghid & Davids, 2013).

The point is, with the pursuit of knowledge – the primary mission of a university – a university educates its academics and students on the basis of free, open and critical inquiry in such a way that they become citizens that can advance a democratic lifestyle. Inasmuch as the public mission of a research university is aimed at fostering democratic citizenry ideals, John Willinsky (2011: 296) cautions us against being too overly optimistic of such a mission. For him, a university's public mission of research and the preparation of democratic citizenship for professional responsibilities on the part of students are increasingly being put under threat by the commercialisation of university practices and knowledge. However, he posits (2011: 306) that succumbing to 'increasing commercialization of scholarly publishing' should not be a reason to abandon how students should think and reason, and universities should remain open to the pursuit of knowledge in a democratic citizenry way.

Next, we show that the cultivation of democratic citizenship seems to be commensurable with the idea of producing a thinking university.

Democratic citizenship as an enabling condition of a thinking university

A thinking university, as has been alluded to earlier and following Amy Gutmann (2003: 194), is not 'exempt from critical questioning'. Gutmann (2003: 199, 208) contends that critical questioning is synonymous with being open-minded and to criticise, which comes close to exercising showing dissent. Yet, open-mindedness, criticality and dissent are important ways in which a democratic citizenry exercises democratic justice: civic equality, equal freedom and opportunity for all (Gutmann, 2003: 209). And, considering that democratic justice cannot be exercised without a deep commitment to critical questioning, it follows that a democratic citizenry cannot do without the virtues a thinking university could cultivate in its teachers and students: a deep ethical commitment to dissent, free (autonomous) expression and non-discrimination (Gutmann, 2003: 2009). In referencing schools of education directly, Giroux (1992: 8), for example, maintains that it is up to leadership structures to

> [R]eclaim the language of substantive democracy, critical citizenship, and social responsibility. Instead of weaving dreams limited to the ever-accelerating demand for tougher tests, account-ability schemes, and leadership models forged in terms of a sterile technicism, such programs can become part of a collective effort to build and revitalize a democratic culture that is open rather than fixed, disputed rather than given, and supportive rather than intolerant of cultural difference. Leadership programs forged in the twin logic of individual freedom and social justice can educate existing and future teachers and administrators to work collectively by refusing the role of the disconnected expert and specialist and by adopting in its place the role of the engaged and transformative intellectual.

For Giroux (1992: 8), educational spaces, such as schools and universities, have to promote nurturing and empowering relations by defending themselves as democratic public spheres that are responsible for providing an indispensable public service to a nation. In this light, a university, following Giroux (1992: 8), needs to be able to awaken the moral, political and civic responsibilities of young people, and also needs to be justified as a space in which students 'are educated in the principles and practices of democracy, not in a version of democracy cleansed of vision, possibility, or struggle'. This implies that a thinking university actually produces individuals as members of a democratic citizenry, intent on fulfilling the promise of democratic justice that grant individuals 'equal freedom and opportunity to live their lives as they see fit rather than to see their identities writ large in their very own society' (Gutmann, 2003: 201). More pertinently, a thinking university can produce individuals who exercise respect for persons. It is respect for persons that allows one to live 'the life of a free person ... free to express one's identity and shape it through one's associations with others' (Gutmann, 2003: 200). For Gutmann (2003: 200), in a just democratic citizenry,

> Free association entails the freedom [of persons] ... to live their own lives as they see fit ... within the limits of doing no injustice to others ... The right of free association ends where injustice to others begin ... [that is] Free association must not become an unconstrained licence to discriminate.

It is important for a thinking university to prevent people from exercising invidious discrimination as that would be contrary to what is expected of a just democratic citizenry. A thinking university cannot be liable for nurturing individuals who discriminate on the grounds of gender, race, sexual orientation, ethnicity, culture and religion as such discriminations in any case 'are unwarranted sources of civic inequality' (Gutmann, 2003: 200). Mutual respect or reciprocity, states Gutmann (2003: 198), entails equal freedom and opportunity. And equal freedom and opportunity, she continues, 'extend well beyond a formal right to leave undemocratic cultural groups that make the cost of exiting exorbitantly and prohibitively high for vulnerable and disadvantaged people ... Respect for human agency requires democracies to grant all individual equal freedoms' (Gutmann, 2003: 198).

The point we are making is that a genuine thinking university supports the advocacy for a just democratic citizenry that does not use its freedom of expression to exclude others on the grounds of injurious speech, for example. Doing so would be tantamount to unjustifiable discrimination and disrespect towards other persons. This is especially evident on university campuses where immigrant students, or students from minority-group faiths, face unprecedented forms of exclusion, humiliation and othering. Studies reveal that one in four students experiences religious intolerance, with Jewish and Muslim students being particularly vulnerable to religious discrimination (Fosnacht & Broderick 2017). In South Africa, students are reluctant to apply to universities due to an increasing climate of xenophobia – both on and off campus (Du Plessis, 2017). For those students, who are marginalised, and who experience inhospitality and hostility, the university space can become one of antagonism and dis-ease, rendering those who already alienated to a silent status of observer. Instead, what a thinking university should be doing is to create opportunities for people to 'come closer to the possibility of mutual respect and reciprocity that paves the way to democratic justice' (Gutmann, 2003: 199). For this to happen, says Levinson (2011: 23–24), students from majority and/or privileged groups 'may need to be taught about the existence and persistence of injustice in society; they may also need to learn that these injustices are partly systemic rather than simply examples of individual wrongs done to others'.

According to Sleeter (2005: 7), allowing for the development of diversity and expertise can serve as an intellectual resource for constructive participation in a multicultural democracy and a diverse world. It is to our benefit, continues Sleeter (2005: 7),

> [T]hat we do *not* all learn the same thing, beyond the basic skills. Helping next generations acquire intellectual resources of diverse communities, including those that have been historically silenced, can enable creative dialogue and work, out of which we might better address problems that seem intractable.

Democracy itself, argues Levinson (2011: 18), is weakened when all students learn only one set of ideas and skills, no matter how inclusive and worthwhile those ideas and skills are. The point, therefore, of cultivating democratic ways of thinking and acting on university campuses and in classrooms is to ensure that the next generation of citizens is equipped to participate actively, engage with others, especially those whose life-worlds are not familiar to them.

Next, we address the concern that a democratic citizenry that is too patriotic can undermine a genuine concern for the freedom to criticise.

On the limitations of patriotism and its implications for a thinking university

If freedom of expression cannot be an unconstrained licence to discriminate against others who are different (Gutmann, 2003: 200), then such a freedom cannot be exuberantly exercised in the name of patriotism. Patriotism is most appropriately linked to an adherence to 'shared national values' and an allegiance to one's own community, such as a loyalty to 'citizens of our own society' and 'citizens of the world' (Gutmann, 1996: 67, 71). For this reason, explains Nussbaum (2002: 9), we neither need to give up our special affections and identifications, whether ethnic or gender-based or religious, nor to think of these as superficial. Our identities, she explains, are constituted by our immediate family, our extended family, neighbours, friends and fellow citizens – based on ethnic, linguistic, historical, professional, gender or sexual identities. For Nussbaum (2008: 79),

> [P]atriotism is Janus-faced. It faces outward, calling the self, at times, to duties for others, to the need to sacrifice for a common good, to renewed effort to fulfill the promises of equality and dignity inherent in national ideals ... And yet, just as clearly, it also faces inward.

From this, we get a sense of the inherent juxtaposition that patriotism might imply a matter of looking inward towards the self, while also looking outward, as the self recognises the self in relation to others. Papastephanou (2013: 170) explains, '[i]nward is the optics of patriotism that focuses on the community, having a vision of improving its laws, regulating citizens' actions, coordinating diverse expectations of social groups within the state, and fulfilling political promises within the community.' 'Outward', on the other hand, 'is the optics of patriotism that faces toward what is located outside the community yet is entangled with it in one way or other' (Papastephanou, 2013: 170). Because we are all part of a bigger circle, which constitutes humanity, 'we should also work to make all human beings part of our community of dialogue and concern, base our political deliberations on that interlocking commonality, and give the circle that defines our humanity special attention and respect' (Nussbaum, 2002: 9).

In agreement with Gutmann (2003), our obligations as a democratic citizenry extend beyond our duties and allegiance to our own national communities and even communities of the world. This is so, on the basis that such communities can be wrong and quite parochial on matters of public interest, and to reduce one's loyalty (patriotism) to such communities' prejudices would be an unjustifiable action. To Papastephanou (2013: 172), 'inward patriotism does not bring about the kind of de-centering of the patriot that leads to critical awareness of outward challenges.'

Giroux (1992: 8) cautions that educating for democracy cannot be reduced to forcing students to say the pledge of allegiance. Instead, the concern should be about constructing a pedagogical and political vision, which recognises that the problems within educational spaces lie in the realm of values, ethics and vision (Giroux, 1992: 8). For this reason, maintains Giroux (1992: 8), educating students to live in a critical democracy

> suggests a view of empowerment in which learning becomes the basis for challenging social practices that produce symbolic and real violence, that make some students voiceless and thus powerless, and that also implicate teachers in forms of bigotry, colonialism, and racism.

Students, continues Giroux (1992: 8), need to learn that the relationship between knowledge and power can be emancipatory, that their histories and experiences matter, and that what they say and do can count as part of a wider struggle to change the world around them.

For instance, if a community of persons shares the view that people should be excluded on the grounds that they belong to a particular religious or cultural group, or migrated from their countries of origin to deny nationals work opportunities in their countries, such a view cannot be accepted as plausible enough. An allegiance to the human responsibility of ensuring justice to all in the world, to recognise that all persons be treated as equals, is far more tenable than expressing one's patriotic allegiance to a particular community, unless of course, such a community stands and acts to advance justice. Gutmann (1996: 69) aptly states,

> Our primary moral allegiance is to no community, whether it be of human beings in our world today or our society today. Our primary moral allegiance is to justice – to doing what is right. Doing what is right cannot be reduced to loyalty to, or identification with, any existing group of human beings.

What follows from the aforementioned is that patriotic loyalty to a group or national shared values would not necessarily enhance 'the well-being of future generations' (Gutmann, 1996: 69). Patriotism, argues Papastephanou (2013: 171), should comprise the outward in expecting patriots to be critical of how their country responds to external affairs in which it is involved. For this reason, one of the primary tasks of a university is to advance democratic citizenship through remaining open to deliberation in and about justice for all in the world. As Papastephanou (2013: 175) contends, while one may love what is one's own, 'one may also love that which is attractive or can become attractive and that which is perfectible through common critical effort and constant vigilance to avoid future degenerations and to correct (as much as possible) past failures.' This, then, is indeed what a thinking university ought to embody, if it is to respond responsibly to practices of injustice.

Summary

This chapter commenced by looking at the public responsibility of a university in relation to the cultivation of democratic citizenship. Close attention was paid to the autonomy of a university in terms of whether it responds to this responsibility or not. We argued that if openness is to be prioritised, then a university has to ensure that the kinds of students it produces are open and critical in their intellectual ventures of knowledge production. We continued by arguing that in its mission of being in pursuit of the truth and justice, a university has to be mindful not only of its teaching practices but also of how it prepares students to be more cognisant of their potential contributions to a democratic society. In this regard, we singled out the prevalence of marginalisation of certain groups of students and the role a university ought to play in ensuring that all voices are included, so that the dominant group might check their bias. We concluded by evoking the necessity of democratic justice, rather than endeavours of patriotic nationalism only. We maintained that is through democratic justice that human regard and justice are made visible.

References

Calhoun, C. 2011. The public mission of the university. In D. Rhoten & C. Calhoun (eds.). *Knowledge matters: The public mission of the research university*. New York, NY: Columbia University Press, 1–33.
CHE (Council on Higher Education). 2013. *A proposal for undergraduate curriculum reform in South Africa: The case for a flexible curriculum structure*. Pretoria.
Derrida, J. 2004. *Eyes of the university: Right to philosophy 2*. J. Plug (trans.). Stanford, CA: Stanford University Press.
Du Plessis, C. 2017. Xenophobia fears: 'Fewer African students enrolling at SA universities'. *News24*, 9 June. Retrieved from https://www.news24.com/Africa/News/xenophobia-fears-fewer-african-students-enrolling-at-sa-universities-20170608 [Accessed 20 February 2019].
Fosnacht, K. & Broderick, C. 2017. An overlooked factor? How religion and spirituality influence students. Paper presented at the Annual Meeting of the American Education Researchers Association, San Antonio, 3 May.

Giroux, H.A. 1992. Educational leadership and the crisis of democratic government. *Educational Researcher*, 21(4): 4–11.
Gutmann, A. 1996. Democratic citizenship. In M.C. Nussbaum (ed.). *For love of country?* Boston, MA: Beacon Press, 66–71.
Gutmann, A. 2003. *Identity in democracy.* Princeton, NJ: Princeton University Press.
Levinson, M. 2011. Democracy, accountability, and education. *Theory and Research in Education*, 9(2):125–144.
Nussbaum, M. 2002. Patriotism and cosmopolitanism. In M. Nussbaum (ed.). *For love of country?* Boston, MA: Beacon Press Books, 3–20.
Nussbaum, M. 2008. Toward a globally sensitive patriotism. *Daedalus*, 137(3): 78–93.
Papastephanou, M. 2013. Cosmopolitanism discarded: Martha Nussbaum's patriotic education and the inward–outward distinction. *Ethics and Education*, 8(2): 166–178.
Rhoten, D. & Calhoun, C. (Eds.). 2011. *Knowledge matters: The public mission of the research university.* New York, NY: Columbia University Press.
Sleeter, C.E. 2005. *Un-standardizing curriculum: Multicultural teaching in the standards- based classroom.* New York, NY: Teachers College Press.
Waghid, Y. & Davids, N. 2013. *Citizenship education and violence in schools: On disrupted potentialities and becoming.* Rotterdam: Sense.
Willinsky, J. 2011. *Rethinking what is made public in the university's public mission.* In: D. Rhoten & C. Calhoun (eds.). *Knowledge matters: the public mission of the research university.* New York: Columbia University Press, 290–314.

5 Towards a university beyond critique

Introduction

A university carries with it numerous associated ideas and symbols, as well as prestige and contestation. Universities are many things to many people – often couched in hopeful pursuits of aspirations and economic gain. But, universities are as much places and spaces of conflict and dissent, as they are producers of knowledge. Students – whether in Cairo, Bangladesh, Yemen, Syria, London, New York or Tiananmen Square – have long played key roles in protests and uprisings. In South Africa, students have always been at the forefront of confronting political, social and economic injustices – both during and after apartheid. Seemingly, the more knowledgeable students become about the world around them, the more they seek to distinguish themselves with profitable skill sets, and the more they are likely to push for the political change of which an education has made them aware (Sanborn & Thyne, 2014: 2). Student protests in South Africa, as is the case elsewhere, have often deteriorated into levels of abhorrent violence – highlighting, on the one hand, deeply ensconced frustrations and anger, and, on the other hand, largely inept responses from university management structures. A need for a deeper understanding of the seeming tension between universities and students is clearly apparent. Instead of blaming one another for either not listening, and/or for the violence, it is necessary for a thinking university to be intent upon cultivating a climate of critique – that is, the ability to analyse and reflect, so that dissent and dissonance do not give rise to violence and alienation.

The university and its inherent volatility

The volatility and unpredictability of a university can largely be ascribed to its political and socio-economic contexts on the one hand, and to its academics and students on the other. The context in which a university finds itself invariably affects its policies, positioning and perspectives and, hence, its history. In South Africa, the divisions put into play through apartheid played out most vividly in the establishment of HEIs, where students were required to attend particular institutions, based on their racial classification – that is, 'African', 'coloured', 'Indian' or 'white'. Bunting (2006: 36) explains that by the beginning of 1985, a total of 19 HEIs had been designated as being 'for the exclusive use of whites', two as being 'for the exclusive use of coloureds', two as being 'for the exclusive use of Indians' and six as being 'for the exclusive use of Africans'. The National Party government maintained that any public HEI in the RSA was essentially a legal entity, a 'creature of the state' (Bunting, 2006: 37). As such, continues Bunting (2006: 32), because higher education was brought into existence by an action of the state, its existence could be terminated by another action of the state, which, in turn, authorised the government decision to restrict institutions to serving the interests of one and only one race group. By implication, an institution designated for 'coloureds' could register a student from one of the other three race groups only if such institution had obtained a permit from the education department to which it was accountable.

Furthermore, permits were supposed to be granted only if it could be shown that the applicant's proposed programme of study was not available at any institution designated for the race group to which he or she belonged (Bunting, 2006: 37). Another key emergence from the belief that higher education were 'creatures of the state', explains Bunting (2006: 37), is that institutions were divided into rigid groups in terms of the functions they were and were not permitted to perform – specifically a distinction between a university, and what the government termed a 'technikon'. Bunting (2006: 37) clarifies the distinction as follows:

> The National Party government believed that it had been able to identify the essence of each of the two types of institutions into which it divided the South African higher education system: the essence of a university was science and the essence of a technikon was technology. It used the term 'science' to designate all scholarly activities in which knowledge for the sake of knowledge is studied, and the term 'technology' to designate activities concerned with the applications of knowledge. It followed from its philosophy of 'essences' that the government at that time believed that universities could not become involved in technology (in the sense of the application of knowledge) and that technikons could not become involved in scholarly activities involving the generation of new knowledge.

Bunting (2006: 32) states that, as a consequence of these distinctions, the primary function of technikons had to be that of training students who would be able to apply scientific (or scholarly) principles within the context of a specific career or vocation. And the primary function of universities had to be that of educating students in a range of fundamental scientific or scholarly disciplines to enable them to enter high-level professions (Bunting, 2006: 32).

The eventual result was a higher education system that was profoundly shaped by racial discrimination and inequalities of class, race and gender that spawned the systemic exclusion and marginalisation of 'black', 'coloured' and 'Indian' people (Davids & Waghid, 2017). Higher education favoured the minority 'white' group, and the apartheid ideology resulted in the establishment of universities that were reserved for different racial groups, both in terms of ethnicity and language. The delineation of higher education catering exclusively for students along racially defined lines collapsed into two diametrically opposed constructions: historically advantaged ('white') institutions (HAIs) and historically disadvantaged ('black') institutions (HDIs). These two types of institutions were differentiated according to academic programming, knowledge production, staff qualifications, student access, opportunities and quality, infrastructure, funding and geographical location that disadvantaged the HDIs (Higher Education in South Africa [HESA], 2014: 9).

The emergence of a constitutional democracy in 1994 introduced a complete overhaul of the higher education system into an integrated, 'single, national co-ordinated system that would ensure diversity in its organisational form and the institutional landscape, mix of institutional missions and programmes commensurate with national and regional needs in social, cultural and economic development' (Department of Education [DoE], 1997: 2.3). By 2001, the colleges of education were either closed or incorporated into the universities and technikons, and the 36 HEIs were either merged, unbundled or incorporated to give rise to 11 traditional (research) universities that offer largely degree programmes, six comprehensive universities (one distance education institution in the form of the University of South Africa [Unisa]) and six universities of technology, which are intended to be vocationally and career-focused. The objective of this reform was to engender a differentiated, diverse and articulated higher education system that resonated with the knowledge and development needs of South Africa and the imperative of achieving social justice (HESA, 2014: 10). Badat (2010: 3) comments that the social purposes of higher education are that it should disseminate knowledge, produce critical graduates, produce and apply knowledge through research and development activities, and contribute to economic and social development and democracy through learning and teaching, research and community engagement.

Despite considerable reforms of the higher education landscape – in terms of student access, in particular – the reforms have not adequately and justifiably addressed the past inequities, more specifically as these relate to the educational, material, financial and geographical elements of the ('white') advantaged and the ('black') disadvantaged. The continued under-developed institutional capacities of historically 'black' institutions must be emphasised; providing access to rural poor and working-class 'black' students and inadequate state support for the historically 'black' institutions to equalise the quality of undergraduate provision compromises their (historically 'black' institutions) ability to facilitate equity of opportunity and outcomes (HESA, 2014: 11).

In addition to the allegations of inadequate state support is the implicit reality that as South Africa transitioned from an apartheid to a democratic state, so, too, new forms of corporate managerialism began to dominate, bringing into tension the university as a public good. With the introduction of corporatisation in order for the university sector to reduce its alleged financial risks, more bureaucratic forms of university governance were instituted at the cost of discrediting democratic governance (Peters, 2007: 160). The extent to which government and universities have sought to pursue social equity and redress and quality in higher education simultaneously, asserts Badat (2010:7), has resulted in difficult political and social dilemmas. These dilemmas and paradoxes have spilled over into a dramatic series of student protests, which saw not only university property being destroyed but a number of examinations and graduations being postponed, and a few universities being temporarily shut down.

The point being made here is that, inasmuch as the university can be misused in becoming an instrument or 'creature of the state', the university can also very easily become lost in political rhetoric and promises. Our interest, therefore, is to consider why critique should be embedded within the ethos and systemic structures of a university, and why critique is necessary for the epistemological, political, social and economic well-being of a university.

Critique as thinking

Critique, as an instance of thinking, has for long been associated with the notion of a thinking university. This is because universities ought to be engaging in systematic as well as spontaneous processes of self-reflection, self-analysis and self-interrogation. Michel Foucault (1988) connects critique with sudden upheavals of thought whereby people – university teachers and students – are provoked to think in and about matters that concern them, and to proffer diverse perspectives on such matters. In a way, Foucault (1988) considers critique as a form of dissonance whereby, say, university scholars reflect freely and in opposition to uncomfortable matters. That is, university scholars are unafraid of subjecting their own ideas and perspectives to scrutiny, and they are equally unafraid of addressing topics or events, which might cause unease or controversy. To Malik (2015),

> The university is a space for would-be adults to explore new ideas, to expand their knowledge, to interrogate power, to learn how to make an argument; a space within which students can be challenged, even upset or shocked or made angry ... To be at a university is to accept the challenge of exploring one's own belief and responding to disagreement.

Malik (2018) therefore argues that education is not a product but a relationship between student and teacher, and a process by which knowledge transforms the individual. Education, he maintains, is about creating critical thinkers whose skill is precisely the ability to challenge ideas that are pre-packaged or ready-made (Malik, 2018).

At least two aspects of critique can be accentuated, which form the basis of our renewed understanding of thinking beyond critique. Firstly, we are cognisant of a Foucauldian view of critique that involves 'neither [the] subjection nor total acceptance' of human perspectives – that is, working with ideas and decisions that bring discomfort, yet one remains 'restive' about such concerns (Foucault, 1998: 154). For example, university managers might be uncomfortable with students' reasons for engaging in protestations; yet, they do not in its entirety disagree or outright reject such actions. Rather, university managers remain restive about that with which they are confronted and in some ways point out the assumptions and ways of thinking that underscore protest actions.

Secondly, Jacques Rancière (2011: 4) offers an account of critique that 'consists in blurring the boundaries ... between the political from the social or the public from the domestic'. In other words, to critique means to 'put into question' but not to unravel something in its entirety (Rancière, 2011: 4). For Rancière (2011: 10), 'putting into question' without unravelling matters of public and domestic concerns in their entirety involves dissociating from established views with the aim to use such views differently – that is, assigning 'a meaning that perhaps was not there and certainly was not obvious at the beginning' (Rancière, 2011: 10). It is this notion of critique as dissensus that is tantamount to thinking that breaks away from considering something as absolutely wrong or disastrous (Rancière, 2011: 11). As aptly referred to by him, 'to practice critique as disagreement [dissensus]' is to think of 'the wrong that cannot be settled but can be processed all the time' (Rancière, 2011: 11). Put differently, practising a critique of dissensus involves tracing back understandings of a concept and, concurrently, looking at descriptions, narrations, metaphors and symbols that constitute such concepts. In sum, whereas a Foucauldian understanding of critique involves being in a state of discomfort and restiveness about concepts and practices, a Rancièrean account of critique involves dissensus and unsettlement.

In both accounts of critique elucidated earlier, the actions of a thinking university cannot be considered aloof from discomfort and restiveness, as well as dissensus and unsettlement. Yet, being provoked by such thinking actions – discomfort, restiveness and dissensus – is a matter of something *outside* of a one's thinking that ought to happen. Being restive and in disagreement, for instance, require not only the actions of teachers but also those of students with whom they might be in disagreement. It is not as if one can be restive or in disagreement without something outside of one being present as well. In this chapter, we want to pursue a different line of thinking. Rather than looking at a university of thinking in relation to critique, we want to examine how such a thinking university would look like beyond the realm of critique. That is, instead of just focusing on the presence of those and that *outside* of a university's thinking, we want to explore what it means to look *inside* of such a university – an idea that invariably invokes the notion of the individual self. This brings us to an examination of a university beyond critique – that is, towards a university of witnessing.

Towards a university of witnessing

An ethics of witnessing is most appropriately elucidated by Giorgio Agamben in his *Remnants of Auschwitz* (Agamben, 2002). In reference to the etymology of the term, 'witness', Agamben (2002: 17) refers to its Latin meaning which has two components: the first is *testis* from which the word 'testimony' derives, and which is most poignantly signified in 'a person who' renders a testimony; and, the second word is *superstes*, which designates 'a person who has experienced an event from beginning to end and can therefore bear witness to it' (Agamben, 2002: 17). Both *testes* (a person who renders a testimony) and *superstes* (a person who experienced something and bears witness to it) underscore what it means to engage in an ethics of witnessing or testimony. Thus, following Agamben (2002), bearing witness is a pronouncement of an event that one both experiences and gives a testimony about from the *inside*. Simply put, whereas critique is a form of thinking from the *outside*, witnessing is a testimony from the inside, that is, on account of a person's own experience. For example, a survivor in a Nazi concentration camp can be said to bear witness when he or she gives an account or testimony of that which he or she had experienced directly or from the inside.

For Agamben (2002: 26), the most important metaphorical figure in the Nazi concentration camps would be the *Musselmänner* (the Muslims) or those in the camps who had reached such a physical feebleness and existential neglect that one hesitates to refer to them as living or their death as death (Agamben, 2002: 44). And, following Agamben, it is the *Musselmänner* who bore witness to the indignity and torture of Nazi genocide suffered by those who had to endure physical extermination during the Holocaust. Of interest to our discussion is the act of bearing witness on the part of the metaphorical figure of the *Musselmänner*. In the first place, bearing witness as a Muslim implies that one submits him- or herself unconditionally to the will of Allah (God) (Agamben, 2002: 45). Secondly, those who had to endure torment and suffering in the concentration camps of Auschwitz have lost all their will to live and all consciousness about death they were about to face (Agamben, 2002: 45). Only by having experienced such horror in the camps could survivors give an account or bear testimony to the inhumanity they have experienced in the camps.

The question is, how does the aforementioned understanding of witnessing extend the notion of a thinking university beyond critique? Whereas dissonance and dissensus are associated with a university of critique, witnessing depends on the position of the insider making claims about his or her experiences and finding a language through which he or she can make his or her experiences known to others. Simply put, critique involves thinking otherwise through dissonance and dissensus. Witnessing implies sharing one's experiences with others in and about that which subjugates one – a matter of bearing testimony to one's individual experiences. Three aspects emerge from such an ethics of witnessing. First, the testimony can be given only by those who have experienced the event or occurrence. Second, the testimony is an acknowledgement that things have unfolded without one necessarily having control of its manifestation. Third, only when confronted with inhumaneness and indignity does the possibility exist that the impossible could happen and that some humans could bear witness to it. For instance, 'the shame felt in nudity is not shame at a lack that one perceives in oneself, but a consequence of not being able to present oneself otherwise, of being exposed in a vision from which one seeks to hide' (Mills, 2008: 90).

In relation to a university of thinking, an ethics of witnessing can bring about the following: only when academics are subjected to the performative game of the neo-liberal university, can they begin to bear testimony about how their scholarship would possibly be undermined. And, when these academics bear testimony to some of the debilitating effects of performative demands – such as to publish to enhance the quantity of outputs, would one be in a position to make sense of one's experiences. Only if such performativity brings the act of university life into disrepute and academics begin to treat one another inhumanely in the sense that competition breeds animosity and enmity, would it become possible for a university of thinking to encourage witnessing. It might then become possible that performative actions might just be surrendered to avoid further academic torment and rancour. In other words, an ethics of bearing witness can do more than critique by avoiding inhumane and unjust human experiences.

Critique only provokes people to think differently on the basis of putting to question and encouraging one another to disagree. Witnessing allows one to tackle the inhumane from *inside* to prevent a thinking university from collapsing into an abyss of deceit, dishonesty, academic perjury and injustice. In our own case, we have witnessed a highly commendable and astute faculty debauch into an institution that dishonours scholarship. Only when such an institution bears witness unto itself does the possibility exist for the institution to rise above its de-meritorious predicament towards that which might again be possible – that is, an institution that engages with dissonance and dissensus towards the cultivation of that which is still possible and perhaps yet to come.

Summary

This chapter started by showing how a university cannot be detached or removed from the society within which it finds itself. It is common for universities to be misused and exploited in enacting or furthering the agenda of the state – as was the case in apartheid South Africa. The irony of the South African story is that, although the context has changed dramatically in terms of policy and ideology, universities continue to find themselves in the midst of what appears to be an ongoing struggle with systemic political, social and economic complexities. We recognise the near impossibility of a clear break between a university and the state – certainly when it comes to matters of student access and fees. It is, however, our view and contention that a university should not be tied to the thinking of a state. That is, through practices of critique, as well as academic freedom, it is possible for a university to step back, to take account or reflect, examine and then to act. In this regard, we have argued for a university, which extends beyond just critique, one of witnessing – that is, a university that is prepared to address and speak out against inhumanity from within its own structures. It is worthwhile to note that as we write this chapter, debates on academic freedom have surfaced with renewed fervour. It would seem to us, particularly, as we observe our state of democracy, that much of the constraint and restriction experienced in universities are coming from *within* universities themselves. A university of witnessing, therefore, is the one that is unafraid of dissonance and antagonism – especially when these come from the inside.

References

Agamben, G. 2002. *Remnants of Auschwitz: The witness and the archive.* D. Heller-Roazen (trans.). New York, NY: Zone Books.

Badat, S. 2010. *The challenges of transformation in higher education and training institutions in South Africa.* Paper commissioned by the Development Bank of Southern Africa. Retrieved from https://www.ru.ac.za/.../The%20 Challenges%20of%20Transformation%20in%20High [Accessed 13 June 2016].

Bunting, I. 2006. The higher education landscape under apartheid. In N. Cloete, P. Maassen, R. Fehnel, T. Moja, T. Gibbon & H. Perold (eds.). *Transformation in higher education.* Higher Education Dynamics. Volume 10. Dordrecht: Springer, 35–52.

Davids, N. & Waghid, Y. 2017. *Educational leadership-in-becoming: On the potential of leadership in action.* New York, NY: Routledge.

DoE (Department of Education). 1997. *Education White Paper No. 3: A programme on the transformation of higher education transformation.* Pretoria: Government Printer.

Foucault, M. 1988. *Politics, philosophy, culture: Interviews and other writings 1977–1984.* L.D. Kritzman (ed.). London: Routledge.

Foucault, M. 1998. *Politics, philosophy, culture: Interviews and other writings (1977–1984).* New York, NY: Routledge.

HESA (Higher Education South Africa). 2014. *South African higher education in the 20th year of democracy: Context, achievements and key challenges.*

HESA presentation to the Portfolio Committee on Higher Education and Training in Parliament, Cape Town, 5 March. Retrieved from http://www.hesa.org.za/hesa-presentation-portfolio-committee-higher-education-and-training [Accessed 20 February 2019].

Malik, K. 2015. *Free speech in an age of identity politics*. Pandaemonium. Retrieved from https://kenanmalik.com/2015/08/13/free-speech-in-an-age-of-identity-politics/ [Accessed 20 February 2019].

Malik, K. 2018. *What is education for?* Pandaemonium. Retrieved from https://kenanmalik.com/2018/03/19/what-is-education-for/ [Accessed 20 February 2019].

Mills, C. 2008. *The philosophy of Agamben*. Stocksfield: Acumen.

Peters, M.A. 2007. *Knowledge economy, development and the future of higher education*. Rotterdam: Sense.

Rancière, J. 2011. The thinking of dissensus: Politics and aesthetics. In P. Bowman & R. Stamp (eds.). *Reading Rancière: Critical dissensus*. London: Continuum, 1–17.

Sanborn, H. & Thyne, C. 2014. Learning democracy: Education and the fall of authoritarian regimes. *British Journal of Political Science*, 44: 773–797.

6 On a university without condition

Introduction

In the previous chapter, we invoked understandings of critique and witnessing on the basis that when a university embarks on practices of questioning and disagreement together with tackling the inhumane from *inside*, this will hopefully extend the professional activities of a university, and hence its capacity to think. In our view, a university that draws on both critique and witnessing to carve out its professional path seems to be closely connected to what Jacques Derrida (2005: 11) expounds on in his fascinating contribution, 'The future of the profession or the unconditional university'. To Derrida (2005: 11), the university is both an 'invisible force' and a 'place of critical resistance'. Following on Derrida (2005), our interest in this chapter is in his enunciation of a university without condition, which holds the promise of an '*unconditional* freedom to question and to assert, or even the right to say publicly all that is required by research, knowledge, and thought concerning the *truth*' (Derrida, 2005: 11).

Resistance and a university

Power, states Foucault (1998: 63), 'is everywhere' and 'comes from everywhere'. It infiltrates society, and the way society is constructed, making it a 'regime of truth' – that is, power decides on the norms that will dictate a society and, hence, is used as both a source and a medium of discipline and compliance. University students, for example, are expected to abide by particular codes of conduct – this is the 'regime of truth' of a university. When students step out of line from that truth – whether it is to question a university's silence on a pervading rape culture, or a university's inertia in relation to the plight of students' poverty and inability to buy books, or a mere questioning of a faculty's assessment practices – the 'regime of truth' is there to remind them of the repercussions of questioning and bringing into contestation.

When a student questions particular assessment practices of a lecturer, the questioning immediately puts into play complex webs of power. When a student contests assessment practices, the student places him- or herself at risk, because the lecturer might interpret the questioning as undermining of his or her authority and power. That is, the lecturer might consider the action of a student to question as exceeding the boundary of 'truth' (complicit behaviour), which ought to govern a student's conduct. And because the student's questioning is interpreted as undermining, as opposed to a pursuit of clarity or the student's own 'truth', the lecturer might decide to penalise the student through awarding lower marks, or treating him or her differently.

Education, as Finefter-Rosenbluh and Levinson (2015: 5) bring to our attention, is a 'decidedly non-ideal sociopolitical practice, embedded in broader non-ideal sociopolitical structures and relationships'. Universities, like schools, they continue, play key roles in 'credentialing and sorting people and groups, in gatekeeping, and in stratifying society along a variety of dimensions' (Finefter-Rosenbluh & Levinson, 2015: 5). To this end, argue Finefter-Rosenbluh and Levinson (2015: 5), universities and schools 'distribute an incredibly powerful positional good – that of education'. To Brighouse and Swift (2006: 474), positional goods 'are goods the absolute value of which, to their possessors, depends on those possessors' place in the distribution of the good – on their relative standing with respect to the good in question'. They explain that the absolute value of a positional good depends precisely on how much of it one has compared to others:

> Allowing inequalities with respect to those goods, on the grounds that the inequalities benefit, or do no harm to, the worse off, makes little sense. As far as positional goods are concerned, the worse off are absolutely worse off – not just relatively so – simply because they have less than others'.
> (Brighouse & Swift, 2006: 474)

Often, at the university where we are based, we encounter students, who feel that by virtue of their race, culture, ethnicity, language or accent, they are already assessed or looked at differently. They believe that different criteria are in use when their work is assessed, and indeed, the assessment has already occurred before the lecturer had read an assignment or examination paper. Similar assertions are made when students try to access universities in South Africa. Their positional goods, or in their case, positional deficits – as in poverty and poor social capital – prevent them adjusting the scales of inequality. Hence, Brighouse and Swift's (2006: 476) contention is that 'the fact that wealthy parents can buy their children educational advantage over others, increasing their marketability and pushing them up the queue for well-rewarded and interesting jobs, unfairly tilts the playing field in their favor.' To them, permitting inequalities in education does not merely benefit some while leaving others as well off as they were before.

Instead, as Brighouse and Swift (2006: 477) maintain, 'the competitive features of the goods in question give them a zero-sum aspect; the mere fact that some have more worsens the absolute position of those who have less.' More simplistically, the fact that some have power – in terms of access and material goods, or in terms of a lecturer deliberately assessing a student differently – means that others have less, or none. As a result, we find the types of upheavals, which underscored the series of student protests, which affected universities in South Africa for close to two years – from 2015 to 2017. As a 'regime of truth' (Foucault 1998, 63), higher education seemingly embodies not only knowledge production but also a pathway out of poverty, and hence autonomy. The power constituted within higher education therefore stems from what it stands to offer, to whom it will make this offer and whether this offer will indeed be sustainable (Davids & Waghid, 2018).

The possibility of power, as a major source of discipline, according to Foucault (1998), implies the possibilities of action and resistance. Resistance to power, Foucault (1991: 75) asserts, is about 'detaching the power of truth from the forms of hegemony, social, economic, and cultural, within which it operates at the present time'. As such, resistance exists within an individual. Put differently, it exists within the student who takes the risk to question or contest what he or she experiences as unfair assessment practices, or within students, who embark on protests against exorbitant university fees. This ensures the retention of positional goods in the hands of a few, while others (who often constitute the majority) are 'absolutely worse off – not just relatively so – simply because they have less than others' (Brighouse & Swift, 2006: 474). It follows, therefore, as Maistry (2014: 63) contends, that citizens who are less capable, for whatever historically determined reason, 'are relegated to barren hinterlands coldly and deliberately demarcated by institutional structures to maintain their subjugation'.

The fact that universities have the power to decide who gains access and who does not, or who receives a bursary and who does not, does not mean that they (universities) should expect that students would or should necessarily comply with their 'regime of truth', or hegemonic practices. Foucault (1997: 292) explains that in relationships of power, 'there is necessarily the possibility of resistance because if there were no possibility of resistance (of violent resistance, flight, deception, strategies capable of reversing the situation), there would be no power relations at all.' Stated differently, resistance emerges because of power; if there is no assertion of power, there is no need for resistance.

Constructions of 'regime of truth' and their accompanying 'positional goods' are both implications of power, and, hence, resistance. A thinking university cannot lay claim to its systemic hegemonic practices, if it is not unconditionally open to those practices of being questioned and resisted. To stifle the potential of student and academic resistance is to be dismissive of an individual's (students and academics, as well as all other university staff) to *unconditional* freedom to question and to assert, or even the right to say publicly all that is required by research, knowledge, and thought concerning the *truth*' (Derrida, 2005: 11). In the ensuing discussion, we pay careful attention to a Derridian conception of a 'university without condition' (Derrida, 2005: 13).

Towards a university without condition

According to Derrida (2005: 13), a 'university without condition' does not exist. Such a university without condition remains 'an ultimate place of critical resistance' and more than critical 'to all the powers of dogmatic and unjust appropriation' (Derrida, 2005: 13). As aptly stated by Derrida (2005: 13–14), in such a university

> [N]othing is beyond question, not even the current and determined figure of democracy, and not even the traditional idea of critique, meaning theoretical critique, and not even the authority of the 'question' form, of thinking as 'questioning' ... [it is a] university without condition: the principal right to say everything ... [that is] the right or duty to say everything ... the right to say everything publicly.

What is crucial about a university without condition is that unconditionality does not constrain a university in saying 'everything publicly' (Derrida, 2005: 13–14). In other words, such a university, more specifically, its teachers and students, cannot be curtailed in their independence – in other words to surrender itself unconditionally, which means that such a university should not be curbed in taking risks in speech and action. For Derrida (2005: 14), unconditionality 'exposes ... the weakness or the vulnerability of the university. It exhibits the fragility of its defences against all the powers that besiege it, and attempt to appropriate it'. Here, we specifically think of limiting the powers of a university to dis-invite scholars not perceived as promoting the democratic ethos of society to render an account of their illiberal views. Dis-invitation or censorship, Malik (2015) argues, has come to be seen as '*more* than the norm'. For many, he contends:

> [C]ensorship has come to be a progressive act, a means of protecting people, challenging power. Restrictions on hate speech, they argue, protect those facing racism or homophobia or misogyny. Restrictions on offensive speech protect the dignity of powerless groups. The use of trigger warnings protect the emotionally vulnerable.

To Malik (2015), the extension of the notion of 'harm', and the idea that almost any form of words or thoughts or ideas can be harmful, has become almost routine in universities. He is adamant in his contention that, to extend the meaning of harm in this fashion, is 'to eviscerate the meaning of the university'. To be at a university, argues Malik (2015), is to accept the challenge of exploring one's own beliefs and responding to disagreement.

A university, which uses its limited power to prevent other scholars from outside of the institution to undermine the democratic values of a university, cannot be categorised as one without condition. As soon as a university is subjected to control by others (such as students, academics or administrators) in order to limit the academic autonomy of others who might hold starkly different views espoused by the university, such an institution would no longer be affirmed an unconditional independence, as Derrida (2005: 15) would argue. For Derrida (2005: 19),

> [The university] demands and ought to be granted in principle, besides what is called academic freedom, an unconditional freedom to question and to assert, or even, going still further, the right to say publicly all that is required by research, knowledge, and thought concerning the truth ... The university professes the truth, and that is its profession. It declares and promises an unlimited commitment to the truth.

In this sense, the responsibility of a university is not only to engage in the pursuit of truth but also to question what and whose truth is being propagated. Equally important to note is Derrida's (2005: 19) deliberate use of the term 'profess', which, according to him, implies 'promising to take a responsibility that is not exhausted in the act of knowing or teaching'.

In principle, a university without condition is constituted by 'a force of resistance – and of dissidence' (Derrida, 2005: 15). This is tantamount to an 'assumed freedom to say everything in the public space ... by way of critique, questioning and, beyond the philosophy of critique and questioning, by way of deconstruction'. This deconstructive agenda of a university is about ensuring justice – a faith in the professional task of a university to enact its public responsibility (Derrida, 2005: 17). By public responsibility, Derrida (2005: 19) means enlarging the rights of humans, and resisting crimes against humanity. In our context, we are reminded of the role of university students in resisting and protesting against the oppression and indignity of apartheid. Similarly, we are reminded of the series of student uprisings in Tunisia, Bangladesh and Tahrir Square in Egypt – commonly referred to as the 'Arab Spring' – who resisted the dictatorial and oppressive conditions of their respective governments, and were prepared to push and sacrifice for political change and renewal.

The question is, what does it mean to enlarge and elaborate the rights of humans, and to resist crimes against humans? Derrida (2005: 19) posits that the rights of humans are figuratively linked to a capability of promising and resisting crimes against humanity. For Derrida, if the latter were to arrive or be present, it would be the emergence and promise of the new humanities within a university. Such a university would then assume 'new responsibilities' that cannot be exclusively academic (Derrida, 2004: 149). As Attridge (2014: 58–59) clarifies, it is not that Derrida undervalues university research and knowledge. Rather, it is that he sees the task of the university as more than the accumulation of facts, and it is the humanities that are able to provide the lead in this wider responsibility. Attridge (2014: 58–59) explains:

> An important part of what we produce in Humanities departments has affinities to the work of art, in that it arises not only out of the discovery of new knowledge but also from the emergence of unpredictable, unforeseen insights, and in that it is embodied not in sets of facts but in writing or other modes of signification which exceed the communication of the merely factual.

On the one hand, Derrida (2004: 153) purports that the responsibility of such a university is to ensure that the rights of those who make up the university (teachers and students) are to open up one risk against another – always risking the 'worst'. On the other hand, the public responsibility of a university's is to engage in provocative reflection to imagine a moral future that is not yet (Derrida, 2004: 155). In the aforementioned sense, the responsibility of a university ought to be two-fold: to take risks and to be provocative-reflective – referred to by Derrida (2004: 151) as '[t]he new responsibility of the thinking [university]'. Such an understanding of a university would extend the responsibility of the university beyond reason, critique and technical and instrumental thinking. Firstly, for university teachers and students to take risks, a matter of exercising their rights as a community of thinking,

> [They] pursue together a reading, an interpretation, the construction of (a theoretical model, the rhetoric of an argumentation, the treatment of historical material, and even a mathematical formalization) ... [they] posit or acknowledge that an institutional concept is at play, a type of contract signed, and image of the ideal seminar constructed, a *socius* implied, repeated, or displaced, invented, transformed, threatened, or destroyed.
> (Derrida, 2004: 102)

The point about the position adopted by university teachers and students is to make new openings towards an unimagined future. If not, why would they invent, transform, threaten and destroy what already exist? They are, in fact, taking risks accompanied by 'a movement of suspicion' (Derrida, 2004: 151). Without being sceptical of this or that matter, a university risks not putting itself and its work to risk.

Secondly, for a university to be provocative and reflective about its responsibility is to address and offer new configurations and responses to ethico-judicial societal problems. According to Derrida (2004: 198),

> This stems in particular from the memory and the anticipation of global cataclysm, from the forerunners of humanity's self-destruction, from phenomena of totalitarianism, of physical and psychological torture, from the withdrawal of certain philosophico-ideological securities, from techno-scientific powers (in particular over life – organ transplants, genetic manipulation, etc.), from the questioning, by philosophy and psychoanalysis, of the traditional axioms of morality and of the law (the value of the subject, of consciousness, of the responsible I, of freedom, etc.) ... A new problematic of right (for example, of what are called 'the rights of man'), of the experience of illness or health,

of the relations between the political and religious, and so forth, is taking shape and everywhere calls for a *different encounter* with the philosophical as such.

For a university to be provocatively reflective, it has to call out for or invent different radical openings to come up with what is not yet – new possibilities that can take a university into the realm of the seemingly impossible. In a way, it is the responsibility of such a new university, one without condition, to invent alternate ways to deal with human torture, migration of asylum seekers and those who perpetrate terror. Only then would such a university act with a renewed responsibility towards a future – a matter of going beyond the profound and the radical (Derrida, 2004: 153). According to Derrida (2004: 154),

> In a period of 'crisis', as we say, a period of decadence and renewal, when the institution is on the blink, provocation to think brings together in the *same* instant the desire for memory and exposure to the future, the fidelity of guardian faithful enough to want to keep even the chance of a future, in other words the singular responsibility of what he does not have and of what is not yet.

In conclusion, Derrida (2005: 23) is well aware that a 'university without conditions does not, in fact, exist.' He recognises that the 'regime of truth' and 'positional good', which affect the functioning and existence of a university, make it nearly impossible for it to exist without conditions, as we know only too well. Nevertheless, Derrida (2005: 23) maintains, 'in principle and in conformity to its declared vocation, its professed essence, it should remain an ultimate place of critical resistance – and more than critical – to all the powers of dogmatic and unjust appropriation' (2005: 23). As such, a university can be considered open and hospitable, 'only if the *un*invited one enters your house and transforms it'. This, according to Derrida, is the 'the real and best source of knowledge' (Manuel, 1999).

Summary

We started this chapter by looking at the pervading climate of power, which occupies the spaces of all universities. By drawing on Foucault (1998), we looked at the implicit co-existence and interplay between power and resistance, and argued that if universities persist in claiming their own truth, then, as thinking universities, they have to accept that students and academics alike have their own truth and, hence, exist in resistance to the 'regime of truth' of a university. At the centre of this chapter is Derrida's (2005) conception of a 'university without condition'. Although Derrida (2005) acknowledges that an unconditional university does not actually exist, and is always constrained by an array of systemic, political and economic complexities, the principle of such a university should stand. And by this, Derrida (2005) has in mind a university that is as open to a reconsideration of diverse truths as it is to engaging with the *'uninvited'*. To him and to us, a 'university without condition' is provocatively reflective because it understands knowledge as being necessarily transformative.

References

Attridge, D. 2014. The humanities without condition: Derrida and the singular oeuvre. *Arts & Humanities in Higher Education*, 13(1/2): 54–61.

Brighouse, H. & Swift, A. 2006. Equality, priority, and positional goods. *Ethics*, 116(3): 471–497.

Davids, N. & Waghid, Y. 2018. Resistance and dissonance in higher education: On doing things differently. *South African Journal of Higher Education*, 32(1): 1–12.

Derrida, J. 2004. *Eyes of the university: Right to philosophy 2*. J. Plug (trans.). Stanford, CA: Stanford University Press.

Derrida, J. 2005. The future of the profession or the unconditional university (thanks to the 'humanities', what could take place tomorrow). In P.P. Trifonas & M.A. Peters (eds.). *Deconstructing Derrida: Tasks for the new humanities*. New York, NY: Palgrave Macmillan, 11–24.

Finefter-Rosenbluh, I. & Levinson, M. 2015. What is wrong with grade inflation (if anything)? *Philosophical Inquiry in Education*, 23(1): 3–21.

Foucault, M. 1991. *Discipline and punish: The birth of a prison*. London: Penguin.

Foucault, M. 1997. *Ethics: Subjectivity and truth*. P. Rabinow (ed.), R. Hurley (trans.). London: Allen Lane, The Penguin Press.

Foucault, M. 1998. *The history of sexuality: The will to knowledge*. London: Penguin.

Maistry, S. 2014. Education for economic growth: A neoliberal fallacy in South Africa. *Alternation*, 21(1): 57–75.

Malik, K. 2015. *Free speech in an age of identity politics*. Pandaemonium. Retrieved from https://kenanmalik.com/2015/08/13/free-speech-in-an-age-of-identity-politics/ [Accessed 20 February 2019].

Manuel, D. 1999. *Philosopher Derrida seeks to 'enlarge, re-elaborate' concept of the humanities*. Stanford report, 21 April. Retrieved from https://news.stanford.edu/news/1999/april21/derrida-421.html [Accessed 27 February 2019].

7 Against the exclusive entrepreneurial university

Introduction

Like any institution, the university, where we are based, has a wide range of strategic policies, which include its vision and mission statements. Specifically, the vision and mission statements of our university read as follows:

> Vision: Stellenbosch University will be Africa's leading research-intensive university, globally recognised as *excellent*, inclusive and innovative, where we advance knowledge in *service of society*.
>
> Mission: Stellenbosch University is a research-intensive university where we attract outstanding students, employ talented staff and provide a *world-class* environment; a place connected to the world, while enriching and transforming local, continental and global communities.
>
> (Stellenbosch University, 2019, our italics)

The university's appeal to excellence and global competitiveness can be viewed almost exclusively, we would say, in terms of an instrumental efficiency. The primary task of a university is to advance knowledge in service of society, which clearly accentuates the drive of the institution to corporatise the university to perform an entrepreneurial role in the service of a public good whereby its knowledge becomes commodified. And, to advance its entrepreneurial capacity further, the university has endorsed a value system that foregrounds 'excellence', 'accountability', 'respect', 'compassion' and 'equity' (Stellenbosch University, 2019). Henry Giroux and Susan Searls Giroux (2004: 277) caution that a university intent on performing only its entrepreneurial role where neoliberalism and a market culture prevail must be challenged if such a university, especially, is going to be reduced 'to the imperatives of hyper-capitalism and glorification of financial markets'. In this chapter, we examine what is wrong with a university in adopting an exclusive entrepreneurial culture, and suggest a way to think differently about a university.

University entrepreneurialism

Neoliberalism, states Harvey (2005), embraces a political economy theory that humanity is best served by promoting individual entrepreneurship in an institutional setting that privileges private property rights, free markets and free trade. In this context, as explained by Parker (2011: 437), a neoliberal philosophy requires government to minimise its involvement and intervention in the operation of free markets. He continues that each individual is said to be responsible and accountable for his or her own actions and well-being, from education, to health and to welfare (Parker, 2011: 438). The burden of individual personal responsibility, contends Maistry (2014: 62), has been deliberately imposed on all members of society, according to which competition is promoted as an acceptable moral value, and incentives drive individual success. Within the prevailing discourse of neoliberalism that has taken hold of the public imagination, asserts Giroux (2003: 180), 'there is no vocabulary for political or social transformation, critical education, democratically inspired visions, or critical notions of social agency to expand the meaning and purpose of democratic public life and its connection to higher education'.

To Harvey (2005), the neoliberal commodification, corporatisation and privatisation of many public assets, financial system deregulation and accompanying speculative wealth redistribution, and the commodification and marketisation of processes, activities, services and relationships have had profound implications for higher education, and specifically for academics. One example, according to Parker (2011: 445), is the way universities 'mimetically respond to and comply with changing societal demands by adapting and indeed radically transforming their educational products to meet student and community demands for vocationally oriented, employment generating programs and courses'. For example, as universities seek to attract and retain revenue-generating stakeholder support, they transform the balance of their educational offerings and research projects, gradually increasing the balance of applied, careerist projects and programmes (Parker, 2011).

In another example, Parker (2011: 444) explains that academics have largely lost their formerly unique roles as independent, professional, expert educators and research scholars operating in collegial association and co-decision-making with their university of which they were members. Instead, Parker (2011: 444) continues:

> They are increasingly being redefined as teaching, research and administrative employees of the university, subject to its strategic objectives and direction, and driven and evaluated by corporate KPIs [key performance indicators] that drill down from university, to faculty, to school, to individual levels. In their performance targeting and measurement environment, academics variously attempt to badge themselves as teaching experts, research managers, degree program development and marketing leaders, or commercial research program development and resourcing entrepreneurs. The academic role definition is therefore more clearly located at the coalface level of university operations, with academics seeking to maximise their KPI results for their own short to medium term benefit and career progression.

Consistent with the centralised managerial decision-making structure and the corporatisation and commercialisation of the university, says Parker (2011: 445), is a reduction in academics' autonomy and freedom of speech. Parker (2011: 445) elaborates that consciously or unconsciously:

> [Academics'] ability to express expert opinions or offer critiques in the public domain, is limited by either their university's management or by themselves, for fear of offending key stakeholders and present or potential funding sources, or by fear of impact on their own performance evaluation, job contracts, tenure and career prospects within the university.

To Giroux (2003: 184), as the boundaries between public values and commercial interests become blurred, many academics appear less as disinterested truth seekers than as operatives for corporate interests. More alarming is the reality, in some cases, of academic research being compromised, as corporations routinely censor research results that are at odds with their commercial interests.

With the blurring of boundaries, entrepreneurialism emerged as a natural corollary of marketisation as some universities sought to broaden their range of activities and diversify their sources of income (Filippakou & Williams, 2014). According to Filippakou and Williams (2014: 72), university entrepreneurialism is linked to the expansion of what is coming to be known as the 'third mission', a catch-all phrase to indicate a wide range of income-earning activities other than traditional degree award-bearing courses, scholarship and scientific research. Third mission, they continue, usually encompasses community service activities 'but is more often linked to income generation through the sale of services of various kinds and hence with entrepreneurialism especially when such activities are new and possibly risky' (Filippakou & Williams, 2014: 72). Hence, we find shifts in language, which, as Biesta (2005: 58) explains, allows for

> [A] redescription of the process of education in terms of an economic transaction, that is, a transaction in which (i) the learner is the (potential) consumer, the one who has certain needs, in which (ii) the teacher, the educator, or the educational institution becomes the provider, that is, the one who is there to meet the needs of the learner, and where (iii) education itself becomes a commodity to be provided or delivered by the teacher or educational institution and to be consumed by the learner.

Our major concern with the idea of an entrepreneurial university, as articulated by Maistry (2014: 68), is that when neoliberal market imperatives drive the education agenda, this agenda clouds the ability to see others as human beings rather than as instruments for profit. Worthy values, such as the ability to think critically and to 'imagine sympathetically the predicament of another person', states Nussbaum (2010: 7), are likely to be eclipsed. Nussbaum (2010: 23) says:

> [E]ducators for economic growth will do more than ignore the arts. They will fear them. For a cultivated and developed sympathy is a particularly dangerous enemy of obtuseness, and moral obtuseness is necessary to carry out programs of economic development that ignore inequality. It is easier to treat people as objects to be manipulated if you have never learned any other way to see them.

To Nussbaum (2010), it is a given fact that students and young people ought to be prepared and educated for democratic participation, so that they are equipped to deal with a diverse society and diverse sets of challenges. Cultivating capacities for critical thinking and reflection, she declares, 'are crucial in keeping democracies alive and wide awake' (Nussbaum, 2010: 10). A thinking university must ensure that young people come to understand 'both the differences that make understanding difficult between groups and nations, and the shared human needs and interests that make understanding essential if common problems are to be solved' (Nussbaum, 2010: 81).

What is wrong with end-oriented research?

From the late twentieth century onwards, states Parker (2011: 434), many universities in developed countries have experienced an arguably exponential rate of change in their environment, structures, strategies and processes. Emerging from a period of relatively sheltered existence, serving predominantly elite and stable national markets, often supported to a large degree by government funding, universities, 'have been launched into a global educational market, and required to generate more actively their own constituencies and resources. Such actions have brought profound changes in their core values, fundamental missions and overall operations' (Parker, 2011: 434). As explained by Neumann and Guthrie (2002: 734), educationists tend to view learning as a process, emphasising understanding and depth of insight. As a learning activity, research is a process whereby academics and higher degree research (HDR) students advance knowledge and understanding of their area. While there are clearly outcomes within this process, continue Neumann and Guthrie (2002: 734), HDR is essentially seen as a 'journey' wherein the undertaking is more important than the completion per se. The authors maintain, '[a] strong outcome focused funding direction does not always sit comfortably in a context where quality of process dominates thinking and behaviour. In the current policy environment however, the quality of research and what students have produced become outcomes' (Neumann & Guthrie, 2002: 734). According to Neumann and Guthrie (2002: 734), within this formula, the university becomes the producer, while students and academic publications become units in the educational process. Echoing the views of Neumann and Guthrie (2002), Parker (2011: 437) asserts that commercial strategies in universities:

> [I]nclude teaching and research becoming translated into calculable revenue generating functions, community linkages and networks exploited for consulting income, intense competition for students and resources, fee charging for educational services, strategic alliances with industry, and aggressive expansion into international markets. Having triggered an entrepreneurial university environment, government has simultaneously retained a high degree of indirect control via oftentimes proliferating performance reporting and accountability systems.

Similar to the bias of our university towards a research-intensive environment that commits its academics and students to scores, inputs and markets – the technical and professional – end-oriented research 'is research that is programmed, focused, organized in an authoritarian fashion in view of its utilization ... whether we are talking about technology, economics, medicine, psycho-sociology, or military power' (Derrida, 2004: 141). Our university has identified 'research for impact' as one of its core strategic themes (Stellenbosch University, 2019). 'Research for impact' seems to be built around prioritising South Africa's nationalised interest of applied or applicable research – that is, end-oriented research. Such an end-oriented research programme – 'research for impact' – seems to be designed for what is 'worthy, or even technically profitable for humanity' (Derrida, 2004: 143). The corporatisation of universities – as is evident in these vision and mission statements of Stellenbosch University – is characterised in terms of culture, governance, structure and operational focus, along with the commercialisation of their missions, objectives and operations (Parker, 2011: 434). Often, 'end-oriented' research is associated with aims that are pledged in advance to some utilitarian purpose – research for impact – at the expense of basic research of which the primary concern would remain the pursuit of knowledge, truth, the disinterested exercise of reason, under the sole authority of the principle of reason (Derrida, 2004: 142).

As noted by Stronach (2011), in recent decades, economic instrumentalism appears to have become the new common sense. As a result, neoliberal economic imperatives such as individualism, competition, commodification of knowledge and the marketisation of education have been driving the strategic direction of education systems across the world (Maistry, 2014: 21). The problem with end-oriented research or research for impact is that it often dichotomises the technological focus, on the one hand, from 'the theoretical, the scientific, and the rational on the other' (Derrida, 2004: 142). Such a dichotomy of knowledges is no longer possible, as aptly remarked by Derrida (2004: 142):

> One can no longer maintain the boundary that Kant, for example, sought to establish between the schema that he called 'technical' and the one he called 'architectonic' in the systematic organization of knowledge – which was also to ground a systematic organization of the university.

For example, at South African universities, over the last fifty years, the discipline of Philosophy of Education – in which we pursue our work – has often been considered as of not much worth for societal impact because of its theoretical and epistemological preferences. According to

Van der Walt (2016: 5), the new official approach to teacher education can arguably be ascribed partly to the general muting of critical scholarship in the humanities and social sciences in post-apartheid South Africa (1994 onwards). Van der Walt (2016: 5) posits that the neoliberal economic revolution driven by utilitarian and pragmatic principles, such as performativity and profit making, also penetrated into the higher education sphere, including teacher education. As a result, he continues, what was once vibrant Philosophy of Education departments at universities, was watered down and offered to the students in the contexts of new subject domains such as Life Skills, Social Studies, Life Orientation and Religion Studies (Van der Walt, 2016). To Maistry (2014: 68), critical thinking and imagination, philosophy and the arts are being replaced with scientific and technical education and testable skills that will enable workplace success. He correctly points out that 'if workplace success becomes the key objective of schooling, it is bound to have effects on curriculum and pedagogy' (Maistry, 2014: 68).

Simply put, it is often erroneously assumed that theoretical insights about education are not always technologically advantageous for schooling. Such an implausible disjuncture between the theoretical and supposedly practical resulted in faculties of education eventually rationalising their philosophy of education departments. Unlike what philosophy of education stands for – an integration between the basic (theoretical) and the practical (end-oriented) – it seems as if attacks on the discipline have been justified mostly because of its end-oriented bias in universities. As Nussbaum (2010: 2) cautions,

> The humanities and the arts are being cut away, in both primary/secondary and college/university education, in virtually every nation of the world. Seen by policy-makers as useless frills, at a time when nations must cut away all useless things in order to stay competitive in the global market, they are rapidly losing their place in curricula, and also in the minds and hearts of parents and children. Indeed, what we might call the humanistic aspects of science and social science – the imaginative, creative aspect, and the aspect of rigorous critical thought – are also losing ground as nations prefer to pursue short-term profit by the cultivation of the useful and highly applied skills suited to profit-making.

Next, we consider an account of how a faculty of education at our university seemed to have succumbed to corporatism or entrepreneurialism.

A corporatist faculty: implications for its scholarly future

Over the last two decades, power in the faculty seemed to have shifted away from scholars to faculty administrators – and here we include the deanship. Roughly speaking, administrative support staff and adjunct part-time faculty staff – to minimise cost implications – outnumber full-time academic staff. The reduction in academic staff meant heavier workloads in terms of teaching and increased supervision of postgraduate students. Despite a reduction in academic staff, research demands – as put into play through a neoliberalist agenda – mean that fewer individuals have to produce more research outputs, which, in turn, attract state funding. In other words, the rate of research publications in a faculty determines the allocation of funding received from government. Adding to the pressure, and the lack of motivation, which might be experienced by academics, is the reality that less than half of the state subsidy allocated to our faculty is for staff remunerations, with the rest being allocated to the overall functioning of the three departments in our faculty.

Like any university faculty, our faculty is challenged by a number of complexities, key of which are staff morale and financial sustainability, which co-exist in an equally intricate web. Academics feel under immense pressure to produce so that the faculty might enjoy some degree of financial stability. At the same time, the stability of the faculty is at risk because the demand for publications is not being met. Some academics motivate and justify their poor productivity levels as an expression of dissatisfaction towards an increasing corporatist university climate. In turn, the university reasserts its neoliberalist stance on the basis of a corporatist survival. As a consequence of what appears to be two competing discourses – one centred on a corporatist ideology of measurable outcomes, and the other on a concern for how we understand the academe and how we come into being as academics – the faculty finds itself unable to move.

For as long as academics struggle with what they experience as untenable corporatist expectations, their academic project remains in limbo. This is evident in the inordinate amount of time spent in faculty meetings and endless debates on numbers, outputs and low staff morale, rather than on academic projects, collaborations and new forms of knowledge. It is equally evident in a number of academics' preoccupation with a performance review, in which higher scores incur higher salary increases. Few, if any, evaluations pertain to quality of work and outputs. Scant attention is being paid to the type of research being produced in our faculty. Our corporatist-based faculty fails to identify and recognise that our scholarly work ought to have a critical and deconstructive function as the attention is only on numbers and scores.

The question is: what are the implications for the scholarly future of the faculty? Firstly, as is evident among many students already, learning to think for themselves is a major challenge. Students seldom question the authority of teachers, and they fail to resist the corporatist orientation of the faculty. Many of them are fairly explicit about their expectations of the university – which is to teach and tell them what they need to know so that they can attain their respective qualifications. As such, the majority of students are mainly concerned with test scores and high percentages – that is, their interest is more on 'accounting than accountability' (Giroux & Searls Giroux, 2004: 276). Students are resistant to any idea that will push them to think, or which will force them to shift out of that which is familiar and comfortable. Every year, in our Philosophy of Education class, we provide students with lists of 'prescribed' and 'recommended' reading lists. We consistently find that only a handful of students would even bother to consult the 'recommended' list. We encounter similar scenarios when students are invited to attend additional seminars or workshops. From this, we infer that students are only concerned with complying with the bare minimum requirements for academic progression; they are not interested in extending their knowledge beyond that which is necessary.

In addition to and in support of corporatist universities, higher education in South Africa relies on the national rating system of the National Research Foundation (NRF):

> The NRF rating system is a key driver in the NRF's aim to build a globally competitive science system in South Africa. It is a valuable tool for benchmarking the quality of our researchers against the best in the world. NRF ratings are allocated based on a researcher's recent research outputs and impact as perceived by international peer reviewers. The rating system encourages researchers to publish high quality outputs in high impact journals/outlets. Rated researchers as supervisors will impart cutting-edge skills to the next generation of researchers.
>
> The rating of individuals is based primarily on the quality and impact of their research outputs over the past eight years, taking into consideration the evaluation made by local and international peers. It identifies researchers who count among the leaders in their fields of expertise and gives recognition to those who constantly produce high quality research outputs. Several South African universities use the outcomes of the NRF evaluation and rating

process to position themselves as research-intensive institutions, while others provide incentives for their staff members to acquire and maintain a rating and give special recognition to top-rated researchers (https://www.nrf.ac.za/rating).

As Morrell (2015: 33–34) explains, research benchmarking in South Africa has historically been associated with two national imperatives: the development of local research capacity and the funding of research. Whether or not an academic has an NRF rating has an influence on a number of prospects, such as promotion and access to research funding. The rating of an academic is public knowledge, nationally, and forces academics to be overly concerned with their own rankings and performance scores, rather than guiding their work to make a difference in society or the academic community for that matter. For Callaghan (2018: 2), the violation of central tenets of the academic process of gatekeeping itself might be considered a violation of academic ethics in that principles of anonymity and confidentiality of identity are not upheld in NRF rating assessments. He explains that an individual applying for rating is not anonymised, unlike in the typical review process, so the applicant is exposed to bias that was not experienced in the blind journal article review methodology. Callaghan (2018: 3) argues that the lack of transparency in the methodology of the rating process creates a potential for harm 'particularly in a context that seems to prioritise research in promotion rather than teaching, notwithstanding the societal imperatives associated with massified higher education and the dramatic inequalities in access to opportunities in our society'.

As academics become more and more preoccupied with complying with corporatist demands in pursuit of promotion and funding opportunities, they are becoming increasingly reluctant to take up positions on controversial issues. Giroux and Searls Giroux (2004: 278) put it aptly when they remark that academics fail to play an active role in 'lessening human suffering ... retreating into arcane discourses that offer them mostly the safe ground of the professional recluse'. Again, Giroux and Searls Giroux (2004: 278) posit the following about 'irrelevant' academics perpetuating a corporatist culture in faculties:

> Making no connections to audiences outside of the academy or to the issues that bear down on their everyday lives, these academics have become largely irrelevant. This is not to suggest that they do not publish or speak at symposiums, but that they often do so to limited audiences and in a language that is overly abstract, highly aestheticized, rarely takes an overt political position, and seems largely indifferent to broader public issues.

The point is subversiveness, critique and witnessing remain elusive from the work of such academics. The pedagogical spaces they create for students seldom bear witness to 'the ethical and political dilemmas that animate the broader social landscape ... [and they do not consistently create] spaces that both disturb and enlighten' (Giroux & Searls Giroux, 2004: 278). In the main, the faculty has become a place where rigorous critical work, even at a doctoral level, is devoid of 'taking of a position' (Derrida, 2004: 102). The majority of these are technically compliant to a set of prescribed rules for interpretation and writing, but often lack the criticality, responsiveness and thoughtfulness to account for something and to play risks off against one another. From our own reading of many theses, we are yet to encounter such works that are underscored by meaningful reflections and provocative thoughts – a sad indictment on the lack of credible scholarship.

Summary

This chapter commenced by looking at the vision and mission statements of our institution. We did this to illustrate the leanings of our institution towards notions of an entrepreneurial university, and to draw attention to the influence of corporatisation on the redescriptions of both the process and the outcome of education. One of the major concerns with an entrepreneurial university, we argued, is that its imperatives are entirely driven by a neoliberal agenda, and the risk of this agenda is that it fails to take into account the human factor and experience. To demonstrate this point, we paid specific attention to our own faculty, where research outcomes-based demands, coupled with a benchmarking process, as manifested in a national rating system, are counter-intuitive to what it means to be in the academe in pursuit of scholarship.

In the next chapter, we shall look at the seminal thoughts of a Muslim luminary, namely Mevlana Rumi. We want to show how some of the ideas in and about a university, as expounded in the preceding chapters, complemented by the thoughts of al-Rumi, can enhance the notion of a university beyond critique.

References

Biesta, G. 2005. Against learning: Reclaiming a language for education in an age of learning. *Nordisk Pedagogik*, 25: 54–66.

Callaghan, C. 2018. A review of South Africa's National Research Foundation's ratings methodology from a social science perspective. *South African Journal of Science*, 114(3/4): 1–7.

Derrida, J. 2004. *Eyes of the university: Right to philosophy 2.* J. Plug (trans.). Stanford, CA: Stanford University Press.
Filippakou, O. & Williams, G. 2014. Academic capitalism and entrepreneurial universities as a new paradigm of 'development'. *Open Review of Educational Research*, 1(1): 70–83.
Giroux, H. 2003. Selling out higher education. *Policy Futures in Education*, 1(1): 179–200.
Giroux, H.A. & Searls Giroux, S. 2004. *Take back higher education: Race, youth, and the crisis of democracy in the post-civil rights era.* New York, NY: Palgrave Macmillan.
Harvey, D. 2005. *A brief history of neoliberalism.* Oxford: Oxford University Press.
Maistry, S. 2014. Education for economic growth: A neoliberal fallacy in South Africa. *Alternation*, 21(1): 57–75.
Morell, R. 2015. Academic benchmarking: South Africa's researcher rating system. In L. Holness (ed.). *Growing the next generation of researchers: A handbook for emerging researchers and their mentors.* Cape Town: UCT Press, 33–41.
Neumann, R. & Guthrie, J. 2002. The corporatization of research in Australian higher education. *Critical Perspectives on Accounting*, 13: 721–741.
Nussbaum, M. 2010. *Not for profit: Why democracy needs the social sciences.* Princeton, NJ: Princeton University Press.
Parker, L. 2011. University corporatisation: Driving redefinition. *Critical Perspectives on Accounting*, 22: 434–450.
Stellenbosch University. 2019. Vision 2040 and strategic framework 2019–2024. Retrieved from http://www.sun.ac.za/english/about-us/strategic-documents [Accessed 1 March 2019].
Stronach, I. 2011. *Globalizing Education, Educating the Local: How Method Made us Mad.* London: Routledge.
Van der Walt, J.L. 2016. Christian philosophy of education in South Africa: The cultural-historical activity theory to the rescue? *KOERS: Bulletin for Christian Scholarship*, 81(2): 1–9.

8 Al-Rumi and the notion of a university beyond critique

Introduction

Mevlana Jalal al-Din al-Rumi. Rumi was born in Balkh, Khurasan in Persia, in AD 1207 into a religious family. After the conquest of Mongol, when Rumi was six years old, the family moved and settled in Konya. Under his father, Baha'al Din, a recognised Sufi, Rumi was exposed to mystical poetry. After his father's death, Rumi, at age 24, assumed all religious duties, and became engrossed with Sufism (Abd Rahim, 2016). Of deep significance to Rumi and his writings were his meeting of Shamsaddin Muhammad-I Tabrizi, or Shams of Tabriz, in Konya, when he was 37 years old. His deep spiritual and emotional connection with Shams changed his path of life from an established teacher and jurist to an ascetic. According to Chittick (1983: 3), Shams Tabriz's had a decisive influence on Rumi – transforming him from a jurisprudent to an intoxicated celebrant of the mysteries of Divine Love. The eventual disappearance of Shams of Tabriz had a profound effect on Rumi, as reflected in his 40,000 couplets in Divan-I Sham-I Tabriz (Aksoy & Tenik, 2002). Rumi's deep outpouring of love for Shams is expressed in his Masnavi, which consists of six volumes (25,700 couplets), encompassing 12 years of work in Anatolia. Rumi died in AD 1273 and is buried in a splendid tomb next to his father, in Konya (Abd Rahim, 2016).

Just a few months after we started with this book, one of us had the privilege and honour to be invited to Necmettin Erbakan University. The university is situated in the serene and cultural city of Konya, Turkey – the burial place of Mevlana Jalal al-Din al-Rumi. It is at the Mevlana Rumi Museum that a copy of Rumi's *The Mathnawi* was acquired. Rumi's works remain organised across various categories:

- The poetry is divided into the Quatrains (Rubayāt), the Odes (Ghazal) of the Divan and the six books of the Masnavi.

- The prose is divided into the Letters (Makatib), the Seven Sermons (Majāles-e Sab'a) and the Discourses (Fihi ma Fihi) (Shahi, 2019).

The Mathnawi is an extensive poem of, in excess of, 25,700 verses. The text not only provides significant insights into Rumi's thoughts but also provides a source through which a renewed understanding of a university beyond critique might be considered. In this chapter, we analyse some of the most salient thoughts of al-Rumi on education and how his thoughts could influence the notion of a university beyond critique.

Rumi and university education

Much of Rumi's work, as Shai (2019: 256–257) observes, contains an ambiguous symbolic representation of his theological visions. Despite this representation, Rumi explicitly warns against a 'strict literalism' in his theological interpretations of the Quran (Shahi, 2019). According to Shahi (2019: 256–257), Rumi questions the supremacy of theology and jurisprudence as unfailing knowledge forms, and openly showcases his unhesitant scepticism towards the academic disciplines of theology and jurisprudence.

In the Foreword of *The Mathnawi*, the mayor of Konya has the following to say extensively about Mevlana Rumi:

> Mawlana Jalaluddin Rumi (1207–1273), better known in the West as Rumi, is one of the greatest spiritual teachers and mystic poets of all times. He stands out like a peak amidst high mountains looking over the vast oasis of human existence. His spiritual message has touched millions of souls and hearts over the centuries.
> Rumi has combined the lore of religion, Sufism and poetry before him with rare perspicacity and eloquence. His life and the Mawlawi tradition which he established are a living testimony to the vibrancy of the spiritual message of Islam. As Rumi says in his Introduction to his masterpiece Mathnawi, his works are nothing but a poetic commentary on the essential meaning of the Qur'an, the sacred book of Islam. In the language of the Sufis, Rumi is a perfect man (*al-insan al-kamil*) who has sung the most beautiful and profound songs of love, compassion and companionship.
> (al-Rumi, 2017: 1)

Our interest is in al-Rumi's enunciations of love, compassion and companionship, and how such thoughts guide higher education. Firstly, in verses 4720–4775 of *The Mathnawi*, al-Rumi (2017: 446) elucidates acts of love in relation to an intelligence that makes one dependent on something or someone else (servitude). Simultaneously, to love also means to act with autonomy (sovereignty), to trust merrily, to be mysteriously flirtatious and to sparkle from inside. What seems to emanate from al-Rumi's enunciation of love in relation to knowledge, is that the one who loves, acts autonomously with trust and wisdom, recognising the mysteries that characterise sources of knowledge, as the one who loves, flirts with his or her encounters and texts in a sparkling (lively) or engaging way. To love, therefore, means to act with independence and trust, but, concomitantly, the one who loves the pursuit of knowledge does so with coquetry and flamboyance so that nothing is left unexamined. It is not that when someone loves knowledge that he or she will ultimately understand everything that is hidden of a person – that is inside, as that in itself is not possible. At least, the possibility exists that something about that which is examined is made to come to some sort of understanding – as al-Rumi (2017: 447) states, what is revealed will 'boil hotly'. Our understanding of al-Rumi's depiction of love should be associated with the pursuit of knowledge for love's sake at a university without condition for the reason that mystery, sparkle and flirtation seem to underscore an examination of that which might be possible yet remains impossible to unravel.

Secondly, al-Rumi's work involves countless references to the act of compassion. One particular genre in *The Mathnawi* that depicts the act of compassion is in the second book under the heading, 'On putting trust in the fawningness and the good faith of the bear'. Here, al-Rumi (2017: 218) relates the story of a dragon pulling a bear into its jaws only to be 'succoured' by a 'valiant man'. The point about this story is clearly related to an act of compassion where a person recognised the grief and helplessness – that is, vulnerabilities – of an animal and felt the need to offer it 'comfort', 'care' and 'help against the dragon' only to have subsequently 'rescued it from the (dragon's) claws' (al-Rumi, 2017: 219). As aptly remarked by al-Rumi (2017: 220–221),

> [T]ake care, do not turn your head away from him that sees the road. You are less (worse) than the bear, for you are not wailing at the pain. The bear was free from pain when it made an outcry. O God, make our stony hearts (soft as) wax; make our wailing sweet (to Thee) and an object of (Thy) mercy.

When a person recognises the vulnerability someone else experiences, and actually does something to address the vulnerability, ensuring the grief and pain of someone else is alleviated, such a person can be described as having acted compassionately. Recognising the vulnerabilities others experience and actually doing something about their discomfort, or shame or misery, is tantamount to acting with compassion – without having the expectation that someone else in return might come to one's rescue should one encounter distress. If we relate such an understanding of compassion to university education, then it follows that teachers should always remain vigilant in recognising the vulnerabilities learning students might encounter. And, when such, perhaps, pedagogical vulnerabilities have been recognised, university teachers are obliged to act in such a way that they relieve the distress and discomfort that characterise students' learning. In a similar fashion, students ought to be taught to be conscious of the plights of others, so that they might act with compassion. In this regard, as Abd Rahim (2016: 112) explains, knowledge should not only be for the benefit of oneself but also be for the benefit and service to others.

Such an understanding of higher education is different to the one espoused through neoliberalist conceptions, where economic gain and risk are constructed as an individual rather than a shared responsibility (Parker, 2011). Higher learning, argues Faust (2009), 'can offer individuals and societies a depth and breadth of vision absent from the inevitably myopic present. Human beings need meaning, understanding, and perspective as well as jobs'. An education which is exclusively focused on individual gain and which is neglectful of a decent world culture creates a tension with what it means to be human and to act with humanity. To Nussbaum (2010: 143), this tension presents

> [A] clash within the individual soul, as greed and narcissism contend against respect and love, all modern societies are rapidly losing the battle, as they feed the forces that lead to violence and dehumanization and fail to feed the forces that lead to cultures of equality and respect.

Following on Rumi, an understanding of higher learning in which the focus is placed on recognition of pedagogical vulnerability with the intent of 'freeing' the other from discomfort is associated with compassionate teaching. This is an approach to teaching–learning that seems to break with the seemingly belligerence associated with pedagogy in many leading universities today. Certainly, in Africa, where vulnerability of students can be associated with having endured oppressive and marginalised moments in their higher pedagogy, acts of compassionate teaching–learning could be considered apt pedagogical moments within which such pedagogy can be enriching and liberating. Often, when vulnerabilities of students are earnestly attended to, such forms of higher pedagogy – especially on the African continent – can be associated with the broader decoloniality agenda. Decoloniality constitutes pedagogical actions that are put into place to reduce and eliminate enslaved forms of university education – that is, education that seems to undermine, indoctrinate and misrecognise the voices of students in particular.

Thirdly, al-Rumi's (2017: 358) depiction of companionship and a sense of community are most appropriately elucidated in reference to his treatment of 'how the seven trees became one'. In his words,

> [A]gain all the seven (trees) became one tree. At every moment they were becoming seven and also a single one: (you may imagine) what I was becoming like, through bewilderment. After that, I beheld the trees (engaged) in the ritual prayers, drawn up in line and (properly) arranged like the congregation (of Moslems): One tree (was) in front like the Imam, the others (were) standing behind it. That standing and kneeling and bowing low on the part of the trees seemed to me very marvelous.
>
> (al-Rumi, 2017: 358)

What al-Rumi seems to explain above relates to the purpose of Muslim prayer: in submission to God (Allah), worshippers stand, bow and kneel down together as being collectively part of a congregation. In this assembly of humans, a leader (Imam) of the prayer initiates the gathering into action as a collective in rhythm: they become one through their engagement; yet, they retain their singularities as they perform the ritual of prayer. The idea of a community in unison is constituted by the singularities of individuals and, simultaneously, the singularities of individuals make up a collective so that the individuals are not alone; yet, they are also not entirely together. Such an understanding of community is of the one that is together with its singularities and, at the same time, the singularities make up a collective. This al-Rumi finds to be a perplexity yet also stunning in the sense that a community (of trees) is at once a collective without abandoning its singularities (separateness as seven individual trees) in much the same way Muslim pilgrims enact seven circumambulations around the Ka'ba in Makkah, in harmony without aborting their individualities or singularities.

To our minds, al-Rumi seems to articulate a concept of community that does not presuppose sameness or distinctiveness as a condition of congregation. The depiction that multiple 'trees' are becoming 'one tree' is a description that allows for the development of community without the announcement of distinctiveness – a situation that is tantamount to humans co-belonging in their singularities. In a way, al-Rumi's conception of community is the one in which all congregate without losing their distinctiveness as individuals. Like the pilgrimage in Makkah, multiple individuals with their singularities assemble on the plains of Arafat in which they momentarily co-belong without completely losing their individual selves. Such an understanding of community where humans co-belong without abandoning their singularities reminds us of Giorgio Agamben's (1993: 86) depiction of a community in becoming in which 'singularities form a community without affirming an identity, that humans co-belong without any representable condition of belonging.'

If individuals do not abandon their distinctiveness and co-belong in community, they do not aspire to be the same as other humans. Rather, they pursue their distinctive identities in a community where they co-belong unconditionally in much the same way worshippers in Muslim prayer perform the act of belonging in congregation, yet they do not lose their singularities as worshippers in prayer. They are bonded in unity by being human to co-belong; yet, they are singular beings like seven trees that appear as one without the possibility of being one. In co-belonging and finding a sense of community within the collective, they are more inclined to act in relation to that community – whether in a compassionate response to another's vulnerabilities, or whether in response to speaking out against injustice. Pedagogically, the idea of co-belonging and feeling connected to a particular community can have profound implications on the educational experience and encounter of students.

At the time of writing this book, an incident unfolded in our Postgraduate Certificate in Education (PGCE) class, which brought into question and conflict the idea of co-belonging and acting in relation to others. One of the academics in our faculty persisted in teaching her particular module in her mother tongue of Afrikaans. In a context of eleven indigenous languages, the issue of language in South Africa has deep-seated ideological and political innuendo and implications – none more so than Afrikaans, which is commonly associated with the language of apartheid, and hence exclusion and non-belonging. In this instance, the persistence of the lecturer to teach in a postgraduate class in Afrikaans is, in fact, contrary to the language policy of the university. The fact that a number of students challenged her on her medium of instruction is unsurprising. What created a deeper problem was that while some students were speaking out against their pedagogical and social exclusion, the rest of the class remained silent. As a result, when one of the protesting students eventually confronted the class by asking why this has become the problem of a few students and not of the collective – given that a policy was being violated, and was therefore an unjust action – she was, in fact, questioning her own position within the collective of the class. She was also bringing into contestation the willingness and capacity of the silent students to think and act compassionately when another was experiencing and witnessing exclusion and non-belonging.

It is unfortunate that this student's articulations revealed a deep sense of a lack of togetherness and co-belonging, brought about by what she has experienced as a lack of compassion and love. The point and learning of this example is that this is just one of countless incidents or encounters, which can arise in any educational setting – known or unknown. A university, based on an ethos of love, compassion and community, remains alert to breaches in this ethos. This is not to say that it would ever be possible to avoid scenarios of this nature – the world in which we live is simply too unpredictable. Rather, universities ought to be geared towards cultivating classrooms where there is less of this happening. In the event where this does happen, students should willing to act with compassion and justice because of an ethical sense of what is right and what is wrong, and because they recognise the vulnerabilities of others.

Now that we have looked at Rumi's conceptualisation of how love, compassion and companionship could affect human relations, we move on to a discussion about why and how such ethical forms of being human could contribute to thinking of a university beyond the act of critique.

A university beyond critique: on love, compassion and togetherness

Firstly, central to the idea of a university is the pursuit of knowledge for its own sake – that is, for the love of it. For Rumi, according to Chittick (2005), the heart is at the core of being human, and from a Sufi perspective, constitutes the innermost nature and potentiality of a human being, and links him or her directly to the world of Spirit. Rumi espouses that the 'fundamental roots of your interior faith and spirituality are of much greater moment than the various branches of jurisprudence and theology' as encountered in the following verse:

> He knows countless chapters of the sciences
> But that wrongdoer does not know his soul

He knows the properties of every essence
But can he tell his own essence from an ass?
'I know what is licit, what's illicit'
But what about yourself? You cannot say
If you're licit or illiterate
(*The Mathnawi*, 3: 2648–56)

Since Sufism refutes the separation between the subject and the object of a knowledge situation, explains Shahi (2019: 266), it (Sufism) 'puts forward an unexplored methodology based on a potential annihilation of a subject–object distinction at the level of consciousness – namely, *baqa wa fana* (literally meaning "subsistence and annihilation", respectively)'. He continues that while '*baqa* denotes the imperfect subsistence of subject into the consciousness of a plural world (object), *fana* implies an annihilation of the subject by passing away into the consciousness of a singular world (object).' For this reason, Sufism considers the combined experiences of '*baqa* and *fana* as an "ongoing process" that gives recognition to both the plurality and singularity (oneness) of reality'. This implies that the quest for knowledge ought to have an intrinsic function – for love of the disciplines – as one cannot revere knowledge without understanding the way in which ideas and concepts evolved through the disciplines, or what Alasdair MacIntyre (2009: 15) describes as 'the nature of the natural and social universe as created and sustained by God, as embodying his purposes'.

The Qur'an – Chapter 3 verse 191 – on which al-Rumi draws for his *The Mathnawi*, emphatically states, *Rabbana ma khalaqta hatha batila subhanaka faqina athaban al-nar* – 'Our Lord has not created this (universe) in vain) – glory to him, the Lord of the worlds.' As al-Rumi (2017) reminds us, love of knowledge for its own sake is connected not only to understanding how they (love and knowledge) manifest in the universe but also to understanding how they are directed by God (Allah). The implication is that any understanding of philosophy, chemistry, genetics and psychology is incomplete without an understanding of God's purposes. Of course, pursuing the disciplines for their own sake does not imply that one does not look at other disciplines. Studying philosophy without any references to physics or history or economics would not be sustained inquiries. As aptly stated by MacIntyre (2009: 17),

> Philosophy is in any case a social and not a solitary form of enquiry. It requires a setting in which different and rival answers to philosophical questions can be proposed and objections to

each considered in detail, so that such answers may be revised or rejected and such objections themselves subjected to critical scrutiny ... Moreover philosophy cannot but draw upon the findings and insights of other disciplines.

Secondly, al-Rumi's notion of togetherness also emphasises that any philosophical understanding of disciplinary knowledge ought to be grasped in relation to other distinctive disciplines and the contributions these disciplines collectively make towards an understanding of the whole. Again, MacIntyre (2009: 146) posits,

> If we were to study each science in isolation from others, or if we were to omit one of the major sciences from the curriculum of teaching and learning, we would go seriously astray both in our understanding of the scope and limits of each particular science and in our understanding of the whole, imperfect as that must always be, the project that gives point and purpose to the activities of a university.

The task of a university of love and togetherness would therefore be to pursue understandings of disciplinary knowledges in relation to one another. As Cardinal John Henry Newman (1982: 94) purports, a university – we would argue, a university beyond critique – 'should foreground philosophical understanding of disciplinary knowledges, arguments and insights through the intrinsic understanding of each of the disciplines and how they connect extrinsically to other disciplines for the enlargement of mind or illumination'.

Thirdly, a university of love, togetherness and compassion 'is intensely focused on solving well-defined problems' (MacIntyre, 2009: 173). This is so because compassion is reflective of an ethical account of a university, whereas love and togetherness are constitutive of advancing a university's metaphysics of inquiry that assents to truth in relation to the nature of God. For a university to act with compassion would, therefore, be 'a way to address the deeper human concerns that underlie its basic problems, without sacrificing depth and rigor' – that is, its love for and togetherness in knowledge (MacIntyre, 2009: 177). The point about a university in compassion is that the pursuit of knowledge cannot be exclusively about finding sufficiently good reasons to advance arguments and debates – that is, the metaphysical. Rather, in addition to addressing matters of metaphysics on the basis of love and togetherness – a commitment to the intrinsic and extrinsic worth of knowledge – a university in compassion directs its concerns for truths towards the ethical as well. As described by MacIntyre (2009: 176), such a university 'articulates and moves toward answering questions the asking of which is crucial for human flourishing'. And, of course, human flourishing, as Walzer (1997) reminds us, emanates from difference and disagreement, in which individual men and women make their autonomy meaningful.

Summary

Referring to Rumi's *The Mathnawi*, this chapter drew on Sufi conceptions of love, compassion and togetherness or companionship, which could affect human relations. We showed how Rumi's depiction of love should be associated with the pursuit of knowledge for love's sake, and as such, remain open to that which is yet to unfold. This was followed by Rumi's understanding of vulnerability, which was drawn on to show that a university recognises pedagogical vulnerability with the intent of 'freeing' the other from discomfort. Such pedagogy is associated with compassionate teaching. Next, we considered Rumi's conception of community, which does not presuppose sameness or distinctiveness as a condition of congregation but co-belong in their singularities. In the second section of the chapter, we argued for a university that extends beyond critique – one which not only advances its epistemological imperative but does so through and for a love of knowledge and, hence, others. A university, founded on love and companionship, we contended, is concerned about the *eudaimonia* or human flourishing of all people, and not simply individual gain and prosperity.

References

Abd Rahim, N.F. 2016. Pedagogical approaches in the light of Rumi: From reflections to integrations. *IIUM Journal of Educational Studies*, 4(1): 100–119.
Agamben, G. 1993. *The coming community*. M. Hardt (trans.). Minneapolis: University of Minnesota Press.
Aksoy, S. & Tenik, A. 2002. The four principles of bioethics as found in 13th century Muslim scholar Mawlana's teachings. *BMC Medical Ethics*, 3(1): 17.
Al-Rumi, J. 2017. *The Mathnawi*. R.A. Nicholson (trans.). Konya: Konya Metropolitan Municipality Culture Publications.
Chittik, W.C. 1983. *The Sufi path of love: The spiritual teachings of Rumi*. Albany, NY: SUNY Press.
Chittick, W.C. 2005. *The Sufi doctrine of Rumi*. Bloomington, IN: World Wisdom.
Faust, D.G. 2009. The university's crisis of purpose. *The New York Times*, Sunday Book Review, 3 September. Retrieved from https://www.nytimes.com/2009/09/06/books/review/Faust-t.html [Accessed 2 March 2019].

MacIntyre, A. 2009. *God, philosophy, universities: A selective history of the Catholic philosophical tradition.* London: Rowman & Littlefield.
Newman, J.H. 1982. *The idea of a university, defined and illustrated in nine discourses delivered to the Catholics of Dublin in occasional lectures and essays addressed to members of the catholic university.* M.J. Svaglic (ed.). Notre Dame, IN: University of Notre Dame Press.
Nussbaum, M. 2010. *Not for profit: Why democracy needs the social sciences.* Princeton, NJ: Princeton University Press.
Parker, L. 2011. University corporatisation: Driving redefinition. *Critical Perspectives on Accounting*, 22: 434–450.
Shahi, D. 2019. Introducing Sufism to international relations theory: A preliminary inquiry into epistemological, ontological, and methodological pathways. *European Journal of International Relations*, 25(1): 250–275.
Walzer, M. 1997. The politics of difference: Statehood and toleration in a multicultural world. *Ratio Juris*, 10(2): 165–176.

9 An argument in defence of a playful university

Introduction

We commenced this book with one question in mind: what are the implications of the notion of profanation on (higher) education? Throughout the book, we have attempted to look beyond the idea of a university beyond reasoning and critique – questioning whether the idea of a thinking university is a sufficient condition for framing the idea of a university. This is not to say that we are doubting a university's capacity or willingness to think. We recognise that it is misleading to attempt to disconnect a university from its epistemological imperative. Rather, our concern is how much of this thinking and acting have been affected by languages of corporatisation, which are steadfast in their foci of 'performativity', 'fitness for purpose' and 'positional goods'. We are concerned about how this singular outcomes-based lens of seeing higher education distorts the humane and ethical nuance of what a university can potentially do and towards which it aspires.

As we conclude this book, we are increasingly sensitive that our concerns might be less directed at the external influences, which compound the complexities of a university, than it might be at the internal discourses and people who collectively come to be what a university looks like. For this reason, we are intent on finding a new use for the idea of a university – one that is responsible and responsive both in its pursuit of the truth and in being open to different kinds of truth, as made manifest in diverse contexts and life worlds. Likewise, we have given consideration to notions of the metaphysical vis-à-vis truth, democracy, citizenship, critique and ethical matters, such as faith, responsibility, love, compassion and togetherness. Yet, our argument has always been to find a different use for the idea of a university – even beyond its entrepreneurial status. In our efforts to profane what a university can or should look like beyond the metaphysical and ethical,

90 *An argument in defence*

perhaps we do not want to mis-recognise the metaphysical and ethical entirely. Rather, we want to examine a new metaphysical and ethical use of a university – one commensurate with the notion of play and playfulness as enunciated by Giorgio Agamben (2007).

The thinking university and profanation

The works in Agamben's Homo Sacer series

- *Homo Sacer: Sovereign Power and Bare Life* (1998);
- *Remnants of Auschwitz (Homo Sacer III)* (2002);
- *State of Exception (Homo Sacer II.1)* (2005); and
- *The Kingdom and the Glory: For a Theological Genealogy of Economy and Government (Homo Sacer II.2)* (2011)

have 'compellingly and persuasively argued that the creating of sacred and sovereign states of exception has often been responsible for the dire states of political affairs we find ourselves in' (De la Durantaye, 2008: 28). Geller (2019) explains that, in the Homo Sacer series, Agamben 'developed the unsettling thesis that everyone subject to the sovereign authority of the modern nation-state has been reduced by a system of biopolitics to naked life, existence devoid of personal dignity and rights'. Being in a reduced state means that people are not legally or morally protected against mistreatment or indignity at the hands of the sovereign.

Moreover, according to Agamben, being reduced to a naked life is not restricted to a small minority but virtually pervasive (Geller, 2019). This is evident in the Holocaust, and in South Africa's apartheid, the Rwandan genocide and the oppression of the Palestinian people. Borrowing from Walter Benjamin (1999), Agamben compares the sovereignty of the modern state as belonging to 'the religious cult of capitalism'; it sacrifices every facet of life through the apparatus of universal commodification and consumption (Geller, 2019). As described by Agamben (2010: 77),

> And yet, in the expression homo sacer, the adjective seems to indicate an individual who, having been excluded from the community, can be killed with impunity but cannot be sacrificed to the gods. What exactly has occurred here? A sacred man, one who belongs to the gods, has survived the rite that separated him from other men and continues to lead an apparently profane existence

among them. Although he lives in the profane world, there inheres in his body an irreducible residue of sacredness. This removes him from normal commerce with his kind and exposes him to the possibility of violent death, which returns him to the gods to whom he truly belongs'.

In response to the above, Agamben offers the text of *Profanations* (2010) in which he considers an antidote to a naked life (reducing the dignity of people), according to Geller (2019). Geller (2019) argues that *Profanations* 'contains developed arguments, suggestions for looking at things differently, critical readings of others' ideas, and a host of personal perceptions, reactions, and reflections'.

According to De la Durantaye (2008: 29), Agamben remarked that profanation is best understood in relation to 'consecration'. 'If consecration was the term that denoted the leaving of the sphere of human law, profanation signified returning something to the free usage of mankind [humankind]' (Agamben, 2010: 83). To profane, therefore, explains De la Durantaye (2008: 29), is to 'return the things that had become subject to a state of sacred exception – things that had been consecrated – to their original context'. Agamben (2010) does not see anything sacred within that which has been deemed sacred. Similarly, he does not conceive of profanation as being synonymous with notions of irreligiosity, disrespect or irreverence. As De la Durantaye (2008: 29) clarifies,

> [Agamben (2010)] sees the sacred as separated from the profane by nothing other than the rituals that set it outside of the continuum of everyday life, thus creating and cordoning off a sacred space and sacred powers to be wielded by the few over the many.

Agamben's interest, therefore, is not to reduce, demean or dishonour. Instead, he views profanation as a positive and pure act, because to profane is to liberate things and to return things to their natural state.

> Profanation, however, neutralizes what it profanes. Once profaned, that which was unavailable and separate loses its aura and is returned to use. Both are political operations: the first guarantees the exercise of power by carrying it back to a sacred model; the second deactivates the apparatuses of power and returns to common use the spaces that power had seized.
>
> (Agamben, 2010: 78)

92 An argument in defence

To illustrate profanation, Agamben (2010: 76) uses the example of play, for which he offers the following motivation:

> The passage from the sacred to the profane can, in fact, also come about by means of an entirely inappropriate use (or, rather, reuse) of the sacred: namely, play. It is well known that the spheres of play and the sacred are closely connected. Most of the games with which we are familiar derive from ancient sacred ceremonies, from divinatory practices and rituals that once belonged, broadly speaking, to the religious sphere. The girotondo was originally a marriage rite; playing with a ball reproduces the struggle of the gods for possession of the sun; games of chance derive from oracular practices; the spinning top and the chessboard were instruments of divination.

Children, explains Agamben (2010), play with whatever falls into their hands. They make toys out of anything, things which we consider trivial, as well as things which hold, at times, serious and disturbing connotations, such as guns and cars. In play, children find new use for things. Consider, for example, how easily a child re-imagines an empty box (often one in which the actual toy had come), so that it becomes a car, a house, a tent, a chair, a table or even space shuttle. The point is that, through play, children find a new use for things. Similarly, Agamben (2010: 77) describes a cat playing with a ball of yarn. 'It consists in freeing a behavior from its genetic inscription within a given sphere (predatory activity, hunting).'

For Agamben (2010: 76) continues:

> [The game with the yarn] liberates the mouse from being prey and the predatory activity from being necessarily directed toward the capture and death of the mouse. And yet, this play stages the very same behaviors that define hunting. The activity that results from this thus becomes a pure means, that is, a praxis that, while firmly maintaining its nature as a means, is emancipated from its relationship to an end; it has joyously forgotten its goal and can now show itself as such, as a means without an end.

In sum, therefore, '[t]o profane means to open the possibility of a special form of negligence, which ignores separation or, rather, puts it to a particular use' (Agamben, 2010: 76).

Now that we have offered some insights into Agamben's (2010) conceptualisation and explication of profanation, we return our focus to a thinking university, this time, with a consideration of what a university at play might look like.

On play and playfulness within a university

Taking our cue from Agamben (2007: 95),

> [Play happens in a] playland or a museum for ghosts (which now often coincide in a single place: the university), but by 'playing' with them, accepts them so as to restore them to the past and transmit them to the future. Otherwise in the face of adults who literally play dead and prefer to entrust their own phantoms to children and children to these phantoms, the shades of the past will come back to life to devour the children, or the children will destroy the signifiers of the past.

Of interest to us is Agamben's depiction of a university as a playland in which the spectres of work with which they play can be linked to the work of people who need reviving; otherwise, they would be devoured. In other words, teachers and students need to play with matters pertaining to a university – such as curriculum, teaching, assessments, learning and debating – else they and their actions would become pointless. When university teachers and students do not begin to play, they would not be in a position to celebrate rituals, manipulate objects and sacred words in and about a university's life (Agamben, 2007: 79). We cannot imagine a university retaining its impetus if it does not revel in research activities in which it manoeuvres traditions, foci and assertions pertaining to the university curriculum.

As philosophers of education, who teach pre-service teachers, we find it incredulous that what we teach would and should not be influenced by the kinds of debates that unfold in our classes or in the broader context of schooling and education in South Africa, and elsewhere. For the latter to happen, we, like Agamben, intimate that teachers and students begin to play. Masschelein and Simons (2013: 37), for example, describe how quintessential artefacts of classical education, such as desk and chalkboard, can be conceived as 'weapons for the disciplining of young people, architecture at the service of pure knowledge transfer, symbols of the authoritarian teacher'. Yet, these artefacts also say something else about the quintessential school.

> The chalkboard that opens up the world to students, and students who literally sit down beside it. Or the teacher who, with his voice, gestures and presence, conjures something from the world in the classroom. Something not only informative, but also enlivening, brought across in such a way that a student cannot help but look and listen.
> (Masschelein & Simons, 2013: 37–38)

When we play with ideas, with teaching methodologies, we try to make sense of which teaching approach would elicit the most levels of engagement. When teachers and students engage in play, teachers disrupt taken-for-granted ideas, expose students to unconsidered ways of thinking, invite students to come to speech (Rancière, 1991) and to actualise their (students) quality so that they might disrupt the chains of reason (Rancière, 2007) and begin to think anew.

Play brings to the work of university scholars, firstly, a 'playland' in which unconstrained 'pandemonium' unfolds (Agamben, 2007: 75). When pandemonium manifests in a university, uproar, bedlam, disorder and subversion of practices emanate (Agamben, 2007: 76). For example, a faculty of education that subverts its academic programme because it constrains student innovation uses play to undermine such a programme. Like children play with toys they manipulate for their own use, so scholars play with a curriculum by subverting established traditions and practices in order to produce other more relevant or provocative spectres of curriculum. Here, we specifically think of integrating the subject of political resistance in every course in post-colonial teacher education programmes at a university. If students can be taught to resist every conceivable aspect of a teacher education curriculum, they would invariably be initiated into a different provocative way of learning, not necessarily indicative of current teacher education curricula in post-colonial Africa. Knowledge, according to Masschelein and Simons (2013: 38), constitutes skills that have a particular function in society, and is free and available for public use. They continue:

> [Subject matter] has precisely this profane character; knowledge and skills are actively suspended from the ways in which the older generation went about putting them to use in productive time, but this subject matter has not yet been appropriated by the representatives of the younger generation.
> (Masschelein & Simons, 2013: 38)

To Masschelein and Simons (2013: 38), the typical scholastic experience 'is exactly that confrontation with public things made available for free and novel use'. Learning to resist politically is an act of play, a discussion we shall attend to in the next section.

Secondly, to resist is also to act with profanation, which means to return things that have been understood in a sacred or religious way – a common way in the past – to a new use (Agamben, 2010: 73). As put by Agamben, '[t]he thing that is returned to the common use of

An argument in defence 95

[wo]men is pure, profane, free of sacred names' (2010: 73). To profane, therefore, means not to abolish or to erase but to deactivate things from an earlier (sacred or common) use and 'to make a new use possible, in order to transform them into pure means' (Agamben, 2010: 87). To put into pure means – to profane or to play – is a matter of rupturing by detaching things from their 'immediate ends' – that is, those ends intended from which have been diverted to make the coming of a new use possible. In this way, Agamben (2010: 92) states, '[t]he profanation of the unprofanable [that which were not thought of as possible] is the political task of the coming generation.' For instance, we are thinking of current forms of educational research that are driven by a quantitative–qualitative divide.

If educational research were to be thought of as sacredly linked to such an unnecessary and indefensible dichotomy as if research in and about human engagement does not involve what can be counted and narrated together, then such forms of research have to be aborted or deactivated and freely put to a new use by educational researchers. For many years now, educational research has been following quite religiously – dogmatically – a way of doing, which is not always encouraging. And, it many cases it fails to reveal the argument, as the immediate end is to ensure that technical procedures and compliance have been adhered to as if research can afford to be remiss of the arguments. To profane, therefore, means to transform the application of educational research politically in faculties of education into a new use – one that is more liberating than previously practised – that is, to make 'coming of a new use possible'.

Thirdly, when a new use for things is imminent, the possibility exists for 'freeing' (Agamben, 2010: 85) an intransigent use of things from its common inscriptions to open them up for a new possible use or play. For long – certainly in South Africa – teacher education has been about making sure prospective teachers are equipped with sacred recipes and technical procedures to maintain discipline in classes or complete lesson preparation plans as if teaching is exclusively about predetermined plans of action, to put into use when they begin their professional careers. Many first-time teachers are trained to enter the profession, often politically unaware of the real contexts within which they happen to find themselves, oblivious or unperturbed about events in schools whether related to racial or transformation issues. Although the content of a number of PGCE programmes at South African universities includes issues of human rights and values, for example, these are often not provided with adequate attention, partly because of curriculum constraints, and partly because of disinterest in the subject, by both teacher educators and students. Commonly, teacher educators are unlikely to focus their teaching on approaches that enable student teachers to reflect fruitfully on experiences of dilemmas and conflicts that arise in their ongoing classroom practices, and quality of reflection is an issue (Orchard & Davids, 2019, in press).

The point is that such teachers do not even begin to see the possibility of a liberatory intent of the teaching profession and continue to think of teaching only in relation to implementing a syllabus. However, much of the work in and about teacher education in postcolonial Africa involves making teachers aware of their responsibility to enhance the democratisation of education in schools, for instance. This is where the concern of profanation with freeing humanity from oppressive situations literally comes into play. The provocation here, argues Lewis (2018), is to think of an educational logic that does not merely result in the socialisation of students into the order of things (as in learning), nor does it merely negate the law (as in certain forms of free schooling), but rather suspends the law of learning without abandoning it.

From an ethics of dignity to an ethics of shame

Following on the aforementioned discussion, Agamben (2002: 69) suggests responding with a new use of ethics – that is, 'a form of life that begins where dignity ends'. If one considers that maintaining dignity is related to a form of 'preserving at all costs' (Agamben, 2002: 69) – i.e. preserving 'the bare life' both internally and externally in the sense that degradation of the human self is safeguarded in public and its decency is protected – then an ethics that does not preserve dignity is different from the one that starts without such a preservation of dignity. For example, the nudity of prisoners in Nazi concentration camps exposed them to shame when their 'dignity and self-respect have become useless' (Agamben, 2002: 63). This new ethics marks the end of dignity, and conformity brings into play an understanding of education beyond dignity and respect. This ethics beyond dignity and respect is the one that is concerned with overcoming resentment and being 'against the spirit of revenge' so that the self is liberated from all guilt and bad conscience (Agamben, 2002: 99). An ethics of dignity demands that humans be treated with respect. But then, such an ethics is pointless if human dignity is visibly violated. The point is that an ethics of dignity is not worth appealing to if its violation is imminent. However, an ethics beyond dignity is the one that preserves the self against resentment and revenge, for the latter will leave the self if enacted with guilt and perhaps a bad conscience.

To rupture the possibility of guilt, an ethics of shame is proposed because it leaves one without guilt; thus, transcending an ethics of dignity (Agamben, 2002: 103). To Agamben (2002: 104), shame 'does not derive, as the moral philosophers maintain, from the consciousness of an imperfection or a lack in our being from which we take distance'. To him, shame is 'grounded in our being's incapacity to move away and break free from itself ... in shame we are consigned to something from which we cannot in any way distance ourselves'. For Agamben (2002: 128),

> [S]hame is truly something like the hidden structure of all subjectivity and consciousness. Insofar as it consists solely in the event of enunciation, consciousness constitutively has the form of something that cannot be assumed. To be conscious means: to be consigned to something that cannot be assumed.

An ethics of shame, therefore, is not about fleeing or evading a wrong situation. Rather, such an ethics is consigned to an event or occurrence from which humans cannot distance themselves. This is perhaps where the decoloniality of education idea is flawed. Decoloniality cannot simply mean the abandonment or omission of coloniality. Such an educational discourse is geared towards appealing to upholding the dignity and respect of the oppressed African peoples.

Such an appeal to an ethics of dignity leaves one with an understanding that the guilty ones who perpetrated coloniality in, for instance, university structures ought to be held to account for having inflicted a wrong on the higher education sector. This was especially evident in the spate of student protests, in 2015, when students resorted to hate speech as a means to call out the historical atrocities, which had been committed against black people during apartheid. But then, it leaves those observing such an act with guilt in the sense that they resent and yearn to avenge the wrongs perpetrated within African higher education. On the contrary, an ethics of shame does not want to evade what wrongly transpired through the coloniality of African higher education and insists on shame in order to break away from the sentiment of revenge and blame on the one hand, and guilt and bad conscience on the other. As Filipovic (2017: 109) explains,

> [Shame] reveals us as willing captives of others but to disclose to others our own infirmities, to finally manifest ourselves in sincerity, is too formidable a possibility. Shame, then, is both the supreme possibility and the utmost impossibility of being oneself. It is auto-affective and dis-affective at the same time, both what signals my being-for myself and my being-for-others.

98 An argument in defence

In sum, for a thinking university, an ethics of shame presents an opportunity for both academics and students to be honest and forthright within themselves. An ethics of shame lays bare the vulnerability of a university; it is attached to certain ways of being and acting, while it is simultaneously forced to take stock of those actions. Within the last year, our institution has begun to commence all major events, such as graduation ceremonies, senate and council meetings, with a preamble, which acknowledges the role of the university in relation to the past, in which it propagated certain segregationist policies, which had led to the harm and hurt of others. To the university, this preamble serves as both an attachment and recognition to what it has done during apartheid, while now also distancing itself from this action. By so doing, the university acknowledges its wrong and shameful actions and affirms its own sense of shame. Through that shame, the university is able to reveal its sincerity in who it now chooses to be. As a result, this enactment of an ethics of shame might create the space and for others to do likewise, whether it is at the level of major atrocities, such as willingly participating in the perpetuation of apartheid, or whether it is an academic, who reveals his or her shame in relation to treating students badly or with discrimination.

Summary

We started this chapter by looking at Agamben's (2010) conception of profanation, which he describes as a positive and pure act, since to profane is to liberate things and to return things to their natural state. As an example of profanation, we turned our attention to Agamben's (2010) play, which according to him, is derived from the spheres of the sacred or ancient rituals. Yet, when children play, they make toys out of anything – whether it is something as problematic as a weapon of war, such as a gun, or an empty box. The point of Agamben's (2010) play is that it puts into action a new use for things, and in so doing, liberates the toy from its original inscription, opening a new possibility. Following on this, we considered a university of play, that is, a university where academics and students come into lively discussion and debate, through which established norms and traditions might be subverted, so that more provocative views might come into being. In this regard, we highlighted the importance of resistance in merely accepting established practices, which are often negligent of particular histories and contexts, which might impede human dignity. This took us to a discussion on an ethics of shame which, according to Agamben (2002), is not about evading a wrong, but rather an attachment and recognition that an individual cannot distance him- or herself from shameful actions. We concluded by looking at our own institution as an example of an institution where an ethics of shame has been adopted into the university's ethos and practice.

References

Agamben, G. 2002. *Remnants of Auschwitz: The witness and the archive*. D. Heller-Roazen (trans.). New York, NY: Zone Books.
Agamben, G. 2007. *Infancy and history: On the destruction of experience*. London: Verso.
Agamben, G. 2010. *Profanations*. Second edition. J. Fort (trans.). New York, NY: Zone Books.
Benjamin, W. 1999. Capitalism as religion. In M. Bullock & M.W. Jennings (eds.). *Walter Benjamin: Selected writings, 1: 1913–1926*. Cambridge, MA: Belknap Press, 288–291.
De la Durantaye, L. 2008. Homo profanus: Giorgio Agamben's profane philosophy. *Boundary 2*, 35(3): 27–62.
Filipovic, Z. 2017. Towards an ethics of shame. *Angelaki*, 22(4): 99–114.
Geller, J. 2019. Profanations. *Notre Dame Philosophical Reviews*. Retrieved from https://ndpr.nd.edu/news/profanations/ [Accessed 3 March 2019].
Lewis, T. 2018. Georgio Agamben. In P. Smeyers (ed.). *International handbook of philosophy of education*. Dordrecht: Springer, 29–38.
Masschelein, J. & Simons, M. 2013. *In defence of the school: A public issue*. J. McMartin (trans.). Leuven: E-ducation, Culture & Society.
Orchard, J. & Davids, N. 2019. Philosophy for teachers (P4T) in South Africa: Re-imagining provision to support new teachers' applied ethical decision-making. *Ethics and Education*, 14(3): 333–350.
Rancière, J. 1991. *The ignorant school master: Five lessons in intellectual emancipation*. K. Ross (trans.). Stanford, CA: Stanford University Press.
Rancière, J. 2007. *Hatred of democracy*. S. Corcoran (trans.). London: Verso.

10 On a university in perpetual play

What we have been arguing throughout this book is that university education cannot remain untainted by new possibilities. It cannot remain fixed in a particular position or worldview, and it has to be open to openness and new considerations, which need to be reflected in its ethos, its academics, research, teaching and, of course, its students. It might be that a university has slacked in its articulation of truths and rationalities, and it could equally be that exclusive critique is no longer what is desired by a playful understanding of a university – especially when one takes into account contexts of neoliberal corporatism. Implicit within our arguments for a playful university is a questioning and subversion of established traditions of a university. This is not to say that traditions and play are irreconcilable. Rather, a university, which is in perpetual play, is able to do new things and find different ways of looking at things, people and ideas. Any university beyond its sacred realities cannot persist with doing the same things over and over again.

Our university, for example, has had to rethink and reflect upon its tradition as an exclusively Afrikaans university – meaning that it catered only for Afrikaans-speaking students. Over time, as the student body of the university transformed from exclusivity to inclusivity and diversity, it became apparent that the 'tradition' of Afrikaans was unsustainable – for very complex, yet straightforward reasons. On the one hand, there was the ideological association of Afrikaans with the language of apartheid – putting into play unresolved tensions for particular communities, whose only experience of this language was one of marginalisation, oppression and displacement. On the other hand, the perpetuation of Afrikaans as a tradition was counterintuitive to the neoliberalist imperative of the university, which speaks a language of globalisation and corporatisation. Afrikaans is not a global language, and is distinctly at odds with a vision that endeavours to establish itself as 'Africa's leading research-intensive university, globally recognised as excellent, inclusive and innovative, where we advance knowledge in service of society', and its mission, which is geared towards attracting 'outstanding students, employ talented staff and provide a world-class environment; a place connected to the world, while enriching and transforming local, continental and global communities' (Stellenbosch University, 2019).

At the time of writing, the language policy had evolved to the point where postgraduate classes should be taught in English, while undergraduate classes are conducted in both English and Afrikaans. What was once considered a foundational and philosophical core of the university has been subverted by time and people – time in terms of a shifting political, social and economic landscape, and people in terms of their diversities, whether linguistic, cultural, racial or ethnic. Of course, the subversion of traditions is never welcomed by all. People generally struggle with change and the unfamiliar. Tradition signifies in a sense of belonging, comfort and safety. When this is altered or removed entirely, people feel threatened and undermined, which is the experience for a few academics within our faculty as we write.

As we have alluded to in the previous chapter, a new possible use of a university cannot be constrained by actions of guilt, resentment and revenge, hence the slow departure of ideas on the decoloniality in university education.

Finding a different use for a university is, therefore, not necessarily a complete abandonment of its past, for what would a university be doing if not constrained by rationality, truth and critique? However, to suggest that a university has an alternative possible use in the realm of the metaphysical and ethical is to nurture its state of 'perpetual becoming', as aptly stated by Ron Barnett (2016: 185). For us, as has been argued, a university's metaphysical and ethical use cannot be constrained only by truth, democracy, rationality and critique, and an ethics of difference and dignity. Rather, the ethical realm of university education ought to invoke notions of shame in order to ensure the allegiance of such university to ongoing play and playfulness. A politics of shame that does not place undignified and disrespectful blame and guilt on others, therefore, ought to extend the ethical realm of a university. It is shame that can contribute towards the quest of a university to pursue the impossible – a matter of reimagining its possibilities, as Barnett (2016: 185) posits.

It is an ethics of shame that moves us beyond revenge, resentment, blame and guilt. Such an ethics put the onus on those affected to come up with possibilities to build a new future without guilt or blame.

They profane and act with playfulness to find new uses for the acts and words of a university beyond the realm of guilt and redress. This is perhaps where universities in Africa continue to struggle and do not get very far in their efforts to transform university education. The problem is that actions, such as transformation, change, decolonisation and decoloniality, are mostly concerned with bringing an ethics of dignity and respect to prevail. It is perhaps time to give an ethics of shame a chance so that we can come up with new possibilities for a university beyond critique, dignity and respect. A politics of shame might just be a renewed possibility of profanation to re-align the metaphysics and ethics of a university.

How then would the metaphysics and ethics of a university in Africa be re-aligned? Firstly, a university beyond critique in Africa should be concerned with 'imaginative ventures' (Barnett, 2016: 97) vis-à-vis democracy, justice, openness, global warming and climate change, the consequences of genetic engineering, historical trauma and memory, artificial intelligence, economics and financial downturn of markets, terror and migration of communities, and so on. In teacher education, we contend that a pedagogy of beyond critique could be relevant for prospective teachers in schools. Prospective or pre-service teachers have to be able to reflect upon who they are, and they have to be able to make sense of how they have come to know what they know, and why. Every year, we encounter students in our classes who believe in corporal punishment as a legitimate form of discipline. Their explanations and justifications are often couched in particular religious, communal or family traditions. They do what they know. Again, unless these traditions are contested and subverted so that students can begin to question why they hold certain beliefs, there is a real possibility and threat that these students will become teachers who use corporal punishment, despite any educational policy which prohibits it. Critique, therefore, should be an unconditional imperative within a university's re-aligned ethics.

Secondly, a university without condition would stimulate teachers and students to embark on contemplation that deals with risks, and what the implications are for audits and curricula assessments. Here, we are particularly concerned about increasing trends of constraints imposed on academics and students regarding freedom of expression, and the types of research on which they embark. A university without condition recognises that it is through the exchange of controversial ideas and debates that new forms of knowledge emerge, which means that free speech has to be unconditional. The significance of this argument is by no means limited to the space of a university. The kinds of constraints, which a university might be inclined to impose, have a bearing on the kinds of students it produces, and hence, on the type of society being cultivated. When students learn that there are certain viewpoints, which should not be listened to, and should be prevented from being articulated, the message they receive is that they do not need to engage with different perspectives and voices. A university without condition is very clear that when academics and students engage with that which is provocative, they learn that what listening demands is not acceptance or agreement with another's argument but the right to allow the other to speak.

Thirdly, a university intent to advocating an ethics of shame should begin to look differently at challenges of transformation and decolonisation and/or decoloniality in relation to pedagogies of teaching and learning. It would seem that the decoloniality project in South African universities is fixated on throwing out that which is considered colonialist, and replacing it with that which is not – referred to intermittently, as indigenous, African or decolonisation. This is not to say that we disagree with the arguments of Mbembe (2016: 32), for example, who asserts

> [There is] something anachronistic, something entirely is wrong with a number of institutions of higher learning in South Africa. There is something profoundly wrong when, for instance, syllabuses designed to meet the needs of colonialism and Apartheid should continue well into the liberation era.

McKaiser (2016) contends that the South African higher education system 'remains a colonial outpost', which continues to reproduce 'hegemonic identities instead of eliminating hegemony'. We are, however, concerned that the emphasis on decolonising the curriculum has meant a neglect of the re-humanising imperative of decoloniality. Here, we are especially concerned about the capacity and willingness of a thinking and unconditional university to detach itself from preconceived ideas and perspectives, and to erase constructions of power, so that what is foregrounded is our collective humanity. A university, which advocates an ethics of shame, should be cognisant of the types of structures and discourses, which perpetuate oppression and exclusion, but should be equally intent on highlighting those ideas and worldviews that have been devalued by hegemonic systems of knowledge and power.

A university in perpetual play cannot be oblivious about its actors – scholars and students – and how they should play. Firstly, the professoriate can no longer keep itself busy exclusively with producing endless encyclopaedias of knowledge on the basis of reading, writing and talking. A university of playland requires that the professoriate begins to proffer (re)interpretations, creations and articulations beyond critique. As one of the representative voices of a university, the professoriate need to be clear what they profess and why. In other words, their scholarship has to be of meaning and significance to advancing the university in its critique, its ethics of shame and its play. Secondly, our re-configured idea of a university is not exclusively the one that abandons rationality and a search for truths. Instead, a university in becoming should adopt more credible habits of reasoning driven by de-sacredised and deconstructed truths of this or that matter. Ideas and conceptions, which are couched in certain traditions, should be questioned – not for the mere sake of contestation or provocation but for the sake of considering renewed ways of thinking and playing.

Thirdly, a playful university should be the one guided by ongoing metaphysical profanations so that pedagogies of discomfort and difference be extended by those of subversiveness and witnessing. Education is not about engaging with that which is familiar; education happens when students and academics alike are able to engage with another perspective, and shifts their thinking – not necessarily towards agreement but towards understanding. Equally, a university of play should extend its ethical enunciations beyond a pedagogy of dignity to one of shame. Only then might we move beyond a university of critique towards one of profanation and play. It would then be a time of 'the coming revolution in [higher] education', as Randall Auxier (2018: 217) intimates.

Rethinking the professoriate at a university of play

If we were to look at the South African example of promotion to a professor, then criteria that would be taken into account in order of priority would be research productivity, postgraduate student throughput at the levels of a master's and the doctorate, rating as a researcher with the National Research Foundation (NRF), international networks and funding opportunities. Seldom, if at all, are questions asked about the credibility of research outputs and the academic voices of postgraduate students. In other words, scant attention is afforded to either the professorial voice or the calibre of students who are produced. The drive by South African professors to gain an NRF rating is so intense that the very idea and process of attaining a rating is seldom brought into dispute. All that matters is the rating. Yet, the NRF relies overwhelmingly on reports from peers to evaluate the level of rating of a person. International reviewers are often unclear about what exactly they need to review, i.e. quantity, quality, credibility or the evolution of an academic voice. This is quite a contentious process because, for instance, irrespective of the low levels of credible outputs of a candidate, whatever reviewers say about applicants are deemed significant enough to the judgement of the NRF.

What concerns us more about the professoriate, especially in the social sciences and humanities at some universities, is that induction into the professoriate happens even without ratings having been acquired by some professors. There are several cases in the higher education sector in South Africa where academics have not produced credible authored books, for instance, yet, they have acquired fairly inflated ratings. However, it is at the level of research productivity that questions can really be asked about professors. One is specifically reminded of publications in noteworthy journals. Yet, when an academic were to publish in lowly rated journals – and here we are not referring to journals with necessarily low citation indexes because some journals might have high impact factors, yet they do not always count as the most authoritative journals in particular disciplines – some of these journals would be used as outputs for academics intent on having their work published. It could be, as is the case in South African universities, that high impact factors are considered necessary for journals to be judged as reputable. But then, this might not always be the case. The point is that some professors happen to publish in journals that do not enjoy much credibility, yet their authority as professors is not undermined.

Recently, there has been the case, and rightly so, of journals recognised as predatory, and some professors hurried to either withdraw articles from such journals or they preferred not to submit articles to such journals. Our position is that the professoriate should be rethought in line with an evaluation of credible academic books that render the authenticity of a professor's voice in and about matters pertaining to higher education. Our motivation is that academic book projects reflect the academic insights of scholars over an extended piece of work, rather than, at times, work captured in rushed articles. The possibility for (re)interpretations, creations and articulations of critique and witnessing might be more possible than in the case of shorter articles. The point we are making is that it seems highly unlikely that a person be deemed a professor with a high rating without even having authored a single international book; yet, there are examples where the latter seems to be the case. What we are intimating is that the professoriate and rating in the country is in need of serious rethinking if it were to be recognised as credible to academic advancement.

Moreover, a university in perpetual play is the one that also rethinks its democratic mission. It can no longer exclusively be about authoritative teachers who insist that students and communities participate in extensive projects to affirm such a university's social responsibility. Rather, communities and students should be summoned to engage with this or that project in order to speak up autonomously and be heard. Summoning them to engage is a recognition that they have something worthwhile to offer and bring to the table. The concern is that many universities consider their service initiatives as extending support in local communities, hence their strategic mission to influence such communities. Such an understanding of instantaneous influence is an approach that considers the role of a university as the one of doing things for communities instead of doing things with them, which is beneficial to both. Similarly, the issue of decolonisation and/or decoloniality has also gained an extreme politicisation agenda. This is so in the sense that decolonisation and/or decoloniality seem to be underplayed as only their political agenda is accentuated to break with the traumatic racist and colonial pasts of African societies.

For us, decolonisation and decoloniality are inherently connected to the democratisation of institutional cultures and structures. Perhaps the play that a university beyond critique should be embarking on is about how notions of democratic education can be expanded to contend with the challenges posed by restricted views of decolonisation and decoloniality. The latter have innate pedagogical concerns to provoke and evoke the potentialities of teachers and students so that they come up with more innovative ways to address issues of change in their communities. But then, decolonisation and decoloniality should be played within more expansive democratic ways.

The majority of universities in post-apartheid South Africa have some intent to reify the significance of achieving dignity for all through the agency of *ubuntu*, that is, a person is considered only a person through others – a matter of human co-existence and interdependence. It seems as if universities feel somewhat compelled to rectify the apartheid wrongs of the past and, therefore, consider cultivating *ubuntu* as a way to account for their responsibility. As alluded to in the previous chapter, the problem with an ethics of dignity or *ubuntu* is that one party wants to ensure that retribution and vengeance and also guilt and blameworthiness be bestowed on another for the sake of rectifying the ills of the past. Such an ethics of dignity is problematic as one party will invariably make the other even more guilty to the extent that even the possibility of respect for the other might disappear, and renewed antagonisms might ensue. Invariably, universities might become places that polarise people instead of bringing them together. Hence, our argument is for an ethics of shame to be cultivated whereby respect and working together would be enhanced without a culture of making the other feel guilty and blameworthy. Of course, those who perpetrated injustices against humanity should be shamed for their acts of wrongdoing, but not to the extent where their guilt and conscience of blame will lead them to withdraw from building a new society.

It would be an ethics of shame that will take universities beyond appealing for dignity and respect. Rather, such an ethics would hold people accountable never to allow shameful acts to recur in the same way. The humiliation of nude prisoners facing genocide should be a reminder of heinous human rights violations that should be shamefully detested. In this sense, a university should remain in a state of play as an ethics of shame only has a beginning where dignity ends, but its potentiality remains ongoing.

Finally, at the time of writing this book, one of us delivered a keynote address at the conference of the South African Council on Higher Education. In the address, one of us who has also recently been appointed as a member of this Council accentuated the importance of theory in relation to quality and quality promotion in higher education. In other words, without an understanding of theoretical constructs in and about quality and quality assurance in higher education, it seems inconceivable that one of the main drivers of quality, namely academic integrity, can be sustained. For instance, the now ubiquitous practice of academic fraud through publications is raising its ugly head in many occurrences ranging from blatant plagiarism of ideas to verbatim copying of extracts from others' published works.

Our contention is that if academic integrity is not going to be practised in terms of the willingness of academics to enrich scholarship, technicist procedures to ensure quality outputs are not going to resolve the predicament of academic decline. Put differently, if academics are not going to hold themselves accountable and remain accountable to the academe, it seems very unlikely that technical policing would counteract any ensuing academic wrongdoing in higher education. Unless the political resistance is there to address academic undermining, and an ethics of blame is constantly pursued where the wrongs of things are seen for what they are without casting blame, scholarship would not be rid of a lack of credibility or quality.

What we have been arguing for in this book can be summarised briefly as follows: a university in perpetual play does not give up on play, and it also does not simply rearrange its toys, such as giving its research a social impact perspective. Rather, a university of play gives its research a different use – beyond the critical and dignified, and its research will bear witness to what is shameful. Such a university would no longer persist in spinning its core functions – research, teaching and learning, and community engagement – in ways that appease a politicised public sphere. Instead, a university of and in continuous play will shape the public sphere in ways that reimagines both the epistemological and the political, and the metaphysical and the ethical. In much the same way that Diogenes, the Greek cynic, gave society a cosmopolitan perspective to look at itself, beyond what is traditional and established towards what is different and unheard of, the time seems ripe for African institutions and scholarship to become sceptical about that which they seem to have been doing for far too long. Long gone are the so-called glory days of Al-Azhar University (in Egypt) and Makerere University (in Uganda), as such institutions have just been carrying on with doing the same things over and over again. Profanation of higher education through play will give universities a different take and edge. For once, universities in Africa might just find their voices again. Such universities would have taken the act of profanation of education more radically and seriously!

References

Auxier, R. 2018. The coming revolution in (higher) education: Process, time, and singularity. In A. Stoller & E. Kramer (eds.). *Toward a philosophy of higher education: Contemporary philosophical proposals for the university.* New York, NY: Palgrave Macmillan, 217–260.

Barnett, R. 2016. *Understanding the university: Institution, idea, possibilities.* London: Routledge.

Mbembe, A. 2016. Decolonising the university: New directions. *Arts & Humanities in Higher Education*, 15(1):29–45.

McKaiser, E. 2016. Epistemic injustices: The dark side of academic freedom. *IOL*, 2 June. Retrieved from https://www.iol.co.za/news/epistemic-injustices-the-dark-side-of-academic-freedom-2029747 [Accessed 5 March 2019].

Stellenbosch University. 2019. Vision 2040 and strategic framework 2019–2024. Retrieved from http://www.sun.ac.za/english/about-us/strategic-documents [Accessed 1 March 2019].

Biographical notes

Yusef Waghid is a Distinguished Professor of Philosophy of Education in the Department of Education Policy Studies at Stellenbosch University. He is the author of *Towards a philosophy of caring in higher education: Pedagogy and nuances of care* (New York: Palgrave-MacMillan, 2019).

Nuraan Davids is a Professor of Philosophy of Education in the Department of Education Policy Studies at Stellenbosch University. Her most recent book is *Universities, pedagogical encounters, openness, and free speech: Reconfiguring democratic education* (2019) (Lanham, MD (US): Rowman & Littlefield – Lexington Series, co-authored with Y. Waghid).

Index

#FeesMustFall 19, 29, 38

academic i, xi, 3–5, 7, 18, 25, 39, 47, 54, 60, 61, 62, 64, 67, 68, 70, 73, 75, 76, 83, 98, 101–105, 107; achievement 26, 28; advancement 105; alienation 25, 26; appointments 5; autonomy 7, 61, 68; book projects 105; books 105; calibre 12; community vi, 75; culture 28, 29, 35; decline 107; demands 26; discernment 4; disciplines 79; environment 25; ethics 75; exchange 7; expertise 6; fraud 107; freedom 18, 19, 55, 61; head space 1, 4; indulgence 1; insights 105; integrity 107; matters 3; needs 3; order 35; performance xi, 26, 28; perjury 54; pipeline 6; process 75; profession 5; proficiency 12; profiles 25; programme 94; programming 49; progression 74; project 12, 73; publications 70; quality 4; rancour 54; rating 75; research 68, 100; resistance 60; responsibilities 5; rigour 9, 10; role 68; scholarship 4; senior 1, 6; staff 5, 6, 73; standards 1; support 28; system 5; torment 54; undermining 107; voice 104, 105; work 1, 5; wrongdoing 107
access 2, 3, 29, 50, 59; demand for 1; democratisation of 2; equal 31; to higher education 2; -ible 2; levels of 39; to opportunities 75; policies of 28; to research funding 75; student 49, 50, 55; to success 2; to university 26, 59
accountability 28, 30, 66, 74; systems 70
act 19, 21, 38, 42, 55, 89, 98, 102; to advance justice 44; anew 20; in attention xii; as authoritative agents 31; with autonomy 80; of bearing witness 53; of belonging 83; of compassion 80, 81, 84; with compassion 81, 84, 86; of critique 84; of discernment 7; of disinvitation 18; of dispair 12; with equality 35; of forgiveness 20; with freedom of judgement 38; with guilt 97; with humanity 82; with independence 80; of injustice 20; of justice 23; with justice 84; with justification 38; of knowing 62; of love 80; of play 94; with playfulness 102; of profanation 12, 108; with profanation 94; progressive 61; pure 91, 98; with reasonable justification xi, 14; in relation to community 83; in relation to others 83; in relation to truth xi, 14; of relieving distress 81; in response 38; with responsibility 64; responsibly 38, 39; of risk 8; of rivalry 8; shameful 107; of thinking 7; unforgivable 22; of university life 54; of wrongdoing 107
advantaged 50; historically 29, 39, 49; institutions 29, 49; universities 39

Index 111

Africa 2, 81; post-colonial 94, 96; sub-Saharan 2
African 48, 102, 103; continent 2, 82; governments 2; higher education 97; institutions 108; peoples 97; perspectives 29; scholarship 108; societies 106; South (*see* South Africa); universities 12, 66, 101, 102, 108
alienation 26, 27, 47; academic (*see* academic alienation); experience of 26, 27, 30, 35; expressing 27; risks of 35; student 26, 28
apartheid: governance 37; ideology 49; indignity of 62; knowledge system 29; language of 83, 100; perpetuation of 98; post- 2, 34, 47, 48, 50, 72, 97, 98, 103, 106; South Africa 54, 90; wrongs 106
argumentation 7; chain of 32; rhetoric of 63; theoretical 9, 10
argumentativeness 7, 10
assessment 1, 4, 58; approaches 28; -driven 4; practices 12, 58, 59; requirements 27; unfair 59
autonomy 18, 59, 68, 87; academic 7, 61; act with 80; capacity for 12; university 18, 45

belonging 28, 90; act of 83; co- 30, 35, 39, 83, 84; condition of 30, 83; marker of 30; non- 26, 35, 83, 84; sense of 30, 101

capitalism: cognitive vii; cult of 90; hyper- 67
censorship 18, 61
citizens viii, 38, 39, 42, 43, 59; actions 43; democratic 38; fellow 43; of our own society 43; of the world 43
citizenship xi, xiii, 37, 38, 89; competency 9; critical 40; democratic xii, 37, 39, 40, 44, 45; education 38
civic: capacities 4; equality 40; inequality 41; responsibilities 41
climate: campus 26; change 8, 38, 102; of critique 47; of power 64; university 73; of xenophobia 42

colonial: outpost 103; pasts 106; post- 94, 96
colonialism 39, 44, 103; institutional 39; needs of 103
coloniality 97; omission of 97
commercialisation 40, 68, 71
communication 28, 63; age of vii; opportunities viii
community 30, 31, 43, 44, 82–84; academic vi, 75; of co-belonging 30, 31; conception of 30, 83, 87; concept of 82; demands 67; depiction of 83; development of 83; of dialogue 43; engagement x, 3, 28, 50, 108; horizons of 20; intersubjective 30; linkages 70; membership 20; of persons 44; responsibility of 38; sense of 82, 84; service 69; of thinking 38, 63; understanding of 82, 83; in unison 82
companionship 79, 82, 84, 87
compassion xiv, 9, 66, 79, 84, 87, 89; act of 80; act with 81, 84, 86; lack of 84; respond with 83; teaching–learning 81; teaching with 81, 87; understanding of 81; university of xiii, 86
consciousness 15, 16, 19, 53, 65, 85, 97; human 15; level of 85
contestation xii, 6, 7, 39, 48, 58, 84, 104
context x, 4, 17, 39, 47, 54, 62, 67, 70, 72, 75, 98; career 49; diverse i, xiii, 89; economic 26; historical 26; of knowledge-production 37; language 83; learning 27; neoliberal corporatism 100; original 91; political 26; post-apartheid 2; real 95; of schooking and education 93; social 26; socio-economic 47; South African 2, 6, 26
corporatisation 3, 12, 50, 67, 68; influence of 76; language of 89, 100; of universities 71
corporatism 72; neoliberal 100
corporatist: conceptions 6; culture 75; demands 75; discourse 4; expectations 73; faculty 73,

74; ideology 73; orientation 74; survival 73; universities 74; university climate 73
credibility 105; of academic voice 105; lack of 107; of research outputs 104
critical 19, 44, 45, 64, 108; awareness 43; citizenship 40; democracy 44; dialogue 7; education 18, 67; effort 45; engagement 4, 10; examination vi, 9; function 74; graduates 49; inquiry 38, 39; intellectual ventures 38; -ity 9–12, 40, 76; notions 18, 67; questioning 40; questions 38; readings 91; reflection vi; resistance xii, 57, 64; scholarship 72; scrutiny 86; thinkers 51; thinking 69, 72; thought 1, 6, 72; work 76
criticism 8, 17, 29
critique vi, vii, viii, xi, xii, xiii, 50–53, 55, 57, 63, 68, 76, 89, 101, 102, 104; account of xii, 52; act of 84; articulations of 105; beyond vi, vii, viii, xii, xiii, xiv, 47, 51–53, 76, 78, 79, 84, 86, 87, 102, 104, 106; climate of 47; as critique 51; as disagreement 52; of dissensus 52; exclusive 100; idea of vii, 60; lines of xii; notion of 52; philosophy of 62; place of vi; practices of 55; realm of xii, 52; sense of vii; theoretical critique 60; as thinking 50; understanding of 52, 57; of the university viii, 19; university of xii, xiv, 53, 104; view of 51; way of 62
cultural 59; city 78; development 49; difference 40; discrimination 41; diversity 101; groups 41, 44; hegemony 17, 59; identity 29; multi- 42; socio- (*see* socio-cultural)
culture 28, 58, 71; academic (*see* academic culture); corporatist (*see* corporatist culture); democratic 40; entrepreneurial xiii, 66; of equality 81; of guilt 107; institutional 3, 29, 30, 106; market 66; of openness 6; rape 57; war vii; of white privilege 29; world 81

curriculum 2, 29, 30, 33, 72, 93, 94, 103; constraints 95; content 28, 30; democratic 29; development 3; redesign 3, 12; reform 30; spectres of 94; teacher education 94; of teaching and learning 86; university xiv, 93

debate 6, 7, 19, 31, 34, 37, 55, 73, 86, 93, 98, 102; ongoing 3; open 38
decoloniality 12, 82, 97, 101–103, 106; agenda 82; of education 97; project 103
decolonisation 102, 103, 106
deconstruction xi, 19–23, 62; concern of 22; Derrida's 20, 23; in education 22, 23; of forgiveness 21; as justice 22; philosophy as 19; philosophy of 20; space of 23; truth and 23; understanding of 20
decontextualised: learner 27, 28
deliberation 3, 4, 18, 19, 31, 34; human 18; open for 32, 44; opportunities for 31; political 43; space of 19; student 4
democracy xi, xiii, 6, 26, 39, 42, 50, 89, 101, 102; boundaries of 39; constitutional 49; critical 44; educating for 43; figure of 60; form of 32; manifestation of 35; multicultural 42; operations of 3; practice for 38, 41; principles and practices 41; state of 55; substative 40; task of 33; version of 41
democratic 32, 34; anti- vii; citizenry xii, 37–43; citizens 50; citizenship xii, 37–40, 44, 45; culture 40; curriculum 29; education 33, 106; encounters 32; engagement 30; ethos 61; exposition of xi; governance 50; justice 40–42, 45; lifestyle 39; mission 8, 25, 33, 34, 106; moments 31, 43; participation 9, 69; politics 33; public life 18, 67; public spheres 40; radical xi; relationships 32; society 45; space of engagement 19; state 50; un- 31, 41; university 28, 31, 32, 34, 35; values 61; visions 18, 67; ways 38, 39, 42, 106

Index 113

democratisation: of access 2; of education 96; of institutional cultures 106
dialogue 6, 7; community of 43; creative 42; critical 7
dignity 43, 61, 96, 97, 107; for all 106; beyond 96; ethics beyond 96; ethics of 96, 97, 101, 102, 106; human 96, 98; in- 53, 54, 62, 90; pedagogy of xiv, 104; of people 91; personal 90; preservation of 96
disadvantaged: education 49; historically 29, 49; institutions 29; people 41, 50
disagreement 2, 7, 52, 87; critique as 52; practice of 57; responding to 51, 61; spaces of 7
discernment 7, 17; academic 4; acts of 7
discourse 27, 79, 103; of academic culture 28; arcane 75; of communication 28; competing 73; corporate 3; corporatist 4; dominant 29; educational 97; interdisciplinary 34; internal xiii, 89; of knowledge 28; of neoliberalism 18, 67; types of 17; of the world viii
discrimination: invidious 41; non- 40, 41, 98; racial 49; religious 42; unjustifiable 41
disengagement 1, 28
disinvitation 18; act of 18; patterns of 18
displacement 100; experiences of 25; sense of 26
disruption: of argumentation 32; of encounters 32; of examinations 39; of ideas 94; of reason 94; student 32
dissensus xii, 33, 52–54; critique as 52; pedagogy of 33, 34; politics of 35; practice of xii; purposes of 31
dissent 11, 40, 47; commitment to 40; enactment of 11; possibility for 11; practice of 11; showing of 40; spaces of 47
dissonance 47, 53, 54; form of 51; unafraid of 55
diversity 49, 100; development of 42

economic: collapse vii; complexity 7, 55, 65; context 26; critical 18; deconstruction (*see* deconstruction in education); democracy 50; development 49, 50, 69; gain 47, 81; growth 69; hegemony 17, 59; imperatives 71; injustices 47; instrumentalism 71; landscape 101; productivity 2; prosperity 9; purposes 2; returns 26; revolution 72; socio- (*see* socioeconomic); stability 37; transaction 69; variation 28; well-being 50
economics 71, 85, 102; sphere of 11
education 4, 8, 22, 30, 33, 47, 51, 58, 67, 69, 72, 79, 81, 96, 104; agenda 69; citizenship (*see* citizenship education); classical 93; colleges of 49; critical 18, 67; curriculum 94; decoloniality of 97; democratic 34, 106; democratisation of 96; department 48; faculties of 72, 95; faculty of 72, 94; higher (*see* higher education); inequalities in 59; institution 49; marketization of 71; outcome 76; philosophers of 93; Philosophy of (*see* philosophy of education); primary 2; process of 69; profanation of 108; programmes 94; quality of 4; reform 2; schools of 40; secondary 2; in South Africa 93; spaces 40, 44; systems 13, 71; teacher 71, 72, 94–96, 102; technical 72; tertiary 2; transformation of x; understanding of xi, 96; university (*see* university education)
educational: advantage 59; discourse 97; elements 50; encounters 11, 22; experience 83; form 33; insights 72; institution 69; logic 96; market 70; offerings 67; policy 102; process 70; products 67; research 95; researchers 95; services 70; setting 84; spaces 53, 56
emancipation 33, 34
encounter 5, 9, 22, 32, 39, 64, 74, 76, 80, 81, 84; deliberative 32, 33; democratic 32; disruption of

32; educational (*see* educational encounters); human 32, 34; pedagogical 4, 31; student 35, 58, 81, 83, 102; undemocratic 31

engagement xii, 5, 6, 16, 18, 25, 27, 28, 33, 40, 42, 53, 61, 63, 82, 103, 104, 106; community x, 3, 28, 50, 108; critical 4, 9; deep 10; democratic 30; dis- 1, 28; with dissonance 54; human 18, 95; intellectual 5; learning 28; levels of 94; need 103; opportunity for 18; pedagogical 25; in play 94; in reflection 63; space of 19, 31; student 4, 31, 32, 94, 103

entrepreneurial: capacity 66; culture xiii, 67; orientation 10; role xiii, 66; status xiii, 89; university xiii, 10, 11, 66, 69, 70, 76

entrepreneurialism 68, 69, 72; university 67, 68

equality 32, 43; act with 35; assumption of 32; civic 40; cultures of 81; factors of 2; in- (*see* inequality); of intelligence 32; practices of xii; promises of 43; of relationships 33

equity 66; facilitate 50; of opportunity 50; question of 2; social 50

ethical i, xiii, 87, 89, 90, 101, 108; account 86; beyond 89; commitment to dissent 40; dilemmas 76; enunciations xiv, 104; forms of being human 84; matters 89; nuance i, 89; realm 101; sense 84; theory 21; use 90, 101

ethics 44, 96, 97, 101, 107; academic 75; beyond dignity 96, 97; of blame 107; of difference 101; of dignity 96, 97, 101, 102, 104; of respect 96, 102; of shame viii, 96–99, 101–104, 107; of testimony 53; of a university 102; of witnessing 52–54

excellence 66; appeal to xiii, 66; research x

exclusion 20, 31, 83, 84, 103; forms of 41; generational 26; historical 26; membership 20; practices of 34; social 83; suffering of 33; systemic 49; tool of 29

experience vii, 16, 17, 28, 29, 32, 44, 52, 53, 55, 59, 70, 73, 75, 80, 84; by academics 73, 101; of alienation 25, 27, 28, 30, 35; combined 85; of dilemmas 96; of displacement 25; educational 83; of feeling held back 27; of forgiveness 22; of health 63; hostility 42; human 54, 76; of illness 63; of the impossible 22; as individuals 17, 53; inhospitality 42; of language 100; learning 31; new 16, 17; of non-belonging 25; others 81; own 54; scholastic 94; student (*see* student experience); of student alienation 28; truth of 16; of uncertainty 26; the world 23

expression 90; of dissatisfaction 73; form of 39; free 40; freedom of (*see* freedom of exspression)

faculty 1, 3, 5, 68, 73, 74, 76, 83, 101; administrators 73; assessment practices 58; astute 54; corporatist 73, 74; departments 73; of education 72, 94; expectations of 26; meetings 73; orientation 74; power 73; staff 73; university 73

faith xiii, 62, 89; good 80; interior 84

financial: downturn 102; elements 50; markets 67; risks 50; stability 73; sustainability 73; system 67

forgiveness 21, 22; act of 20; deconstruction of 21; exercise of 21; pronouncements on 20; subversion of 21; unconditional 21, 22

free 94, 95; to 81, 87, 95; association 41; a behavior 92; break 109; citizens 38; debate 38; from discomfort 52, 81, 87; expression 40, 41; humanity 96; inquiry 39; from itself 97; markets 67; from pain 80; person 41; reflection 51; of sacred names 95; schooling 96; speech 102; trade 67; un- 31; use 91, 94

freedom 7, 42, 63; abandonment of 18; academic 18, 19, 55, 61; assumed 62; communicative 31,

35; to criticise 42; equal 40, 41; to exercise judgements 18; of expression 19, 41, 42, 102; individual 40; of judgement 7, 17, 18, 38; of persons 41; scope of 3; of speech 68; to teach 7, 18; unconditional xiii, 57, 60, 61

head space 1, 4, 8; academic 1, 4; devoid of 1; to engage 4; lack of 1; shrinking 1; of the university 4
higher education vii, 2–4, 6, 9, 18, 22, 26, 29, 33, 48–50, 59, 79, 81, 89, 104, 105, 107; access to 2; African 97; attainment 9; capacity 26; connection to 67; culture 3; demand 2; democratic 34; experienced vii; function of 3; implications for 67; institutions 3; landscape 29, 50; massification 25, 26, 75; opportunities 2; organisational environment 29; practice in 28; profanation of 89, 108; quality 63; reform 2, 29, 50; regulation of 4; revolution 104; role 2; sector 97, 105; social purposes 49; South African 29, 49, 74, 103, 105; sphere 72; students 26, 27; system(s) 2, 3, 48, 49, 103; worldview 29
hostility 7, 42; notion of 7
human 7, 54, 81, 82, 84, 96, 97; -affected issues 30; agency 41; being 43, 44, 69; beings 18, 81; co-belonging 30, 83; co-existence 106; concerns 86; consciousness 15; deliberation 18; dignity 98; encounters 32, 34; engagement 18, 95; existence 79; experiences 54; factor 76; flourishing xiii, 87; imagination 15; injustice against 107; interests 69; issues 3; law 91; living 8; needs 69; perspectives 51; regard 45; relations 84, 87; responsibility 44; rights 62, 95, 107; sciences 16; self 96; suffering 75; thought 29; torture 64
humanity 11, 18, 43, 62, 63, 67, 71, 96; collective 103; crimes against 62; free 96; in- (*see* inhumanity); injustices against 107; new 62

identity 30, 41, 43; affirming 30, 83; annonymity of 75; common 30; confidentiality of 75; culturally defined 29; distinctive 83; ethnic 43; gender 43; hegemonic 103; historical 43; linguistic 43; professional 43; sexual 43; of a university 28
inclusivity 28, 34, 100
independence 18, 60; act with 80; new found 26; unconditional 61
inequality 33, 58, 69; of access 2, 75; civic 41; of class 49; dramatic 88; in education 59; factors of 2; past 2; scales of 59; social 2
inhumane 54, 55, 57
inhumanity 53
injustice 41, 42, 54, 83; academic 67; act of 20; economic 47; against humanity 107; past 20; persistence of 42; political 47; practices of 45; social 47; in society 42
innovation 5, 37; research based 9; student 94; technological 8
institution xiii, 1, 6, 9, 28, 29, 33, 48, 54, 61, 64, 66, 76, 98, 99, 108; advantaged 49; African 108; black 50; capacities 50; disadvantaged 49; distance education 49; educational 49, 69; fabric of 3; higher education 3; of higher learning 103; historically advantaged 29, 39, 49; historically black 50; historically disadvantaged 29, 49; hybrid 9; new 1; of play i, xi; research-intensive 75; thinking x; of thinking 14; type of 48; white 30, 48
institutional: advantaged 29; capacities 50; colonialism 39; concept 63; culture 3, 28–30, 106; disadvantaged 29; drive xiii, 66; environment 30; events 33; landscape 49; missions 49; programmes 49; progress 29; relationship 3; relevance x; setting 67; structures 59
integrity 7; academic 107; principles of 9; of research 9
intelligence 32, 80; artificial 102; equal 31, 32; equality of 32

judgement xii, 6, 7, 18, 33, 34, 37, 105; exercise 18; freedom of 7, 18, 38; plausible xi; rigorous 17
justice xi, 3, 22, 23, 39, 44, 45, 62, 84, 102; act of vii, 22; for all 44; allegiance to 44; democratic 40–42, 45; pursuit of 45; social xi, 40, 49; truth and 45
justification 14, 15, 21, 32, 38, 102; act with 38; framework of 15; reasonable xi, 14

knowledge vii, viii, xii, xiii, 3, 6, 7, 14, 15, 17, 25, 28, 31, 38, 40, 44, 48, 49, 51, 57, 60–62, 65, 66, 80, 81, 85, 86, 94; -able 6, 47; advancement xiii, 66, 70, 101; applications of 48; authoritative 38; based 9; canons of 2; commodification of 71; commodified xiii, 66; and development 49; dichotomy of 84; disciplinary xiii, 86; discourse of 28; dispense 5; dissemination 49; encyclopaedias of xiv, 104; extention 74; forms 79; forms of 7, 14, 16, 26, 73, 102; generation of 48; impartation 14; love of 85, 87; mercantilisation of 10; needs 9, 62; new 48, 62; new forms 7, 73; organization 71; and power 103; procedural 14; producers of 47; production 12, 37, 38, 45, 49, 59; propositional 14, 15; public 75; pure 93; pursuit of 39, 40, 71, 80, 84, 86, 87; quest for 85; of reasons 16; resources vii; situation 85; society 8, 9, 12; source of 64, 80; spectres of xiv; statement 15; system 29; systems of 103; transfer 93; transformation 51; transmission 2; and truth 23; type of 4; university xiii, 52; worth of 86

language 20, 49, 53, 58, 69, 75, 100; of apartheid 83, 100; of corporatisation 89, 100; experience of 100; global 100; of globalisation 100; indigenous 83; of managerialism 1; new 34; of performativity 1; policy 83, 101; in South Africa 83; of substantive democracy 40; of the Sufis 79
learner 27, 69; decontextualised 27; estrangement 27; needs of 69
learning 27–31, 44, 70, 74, 84, 86, 94, 96; activity 70; blended 4, 5; collaborative 30; communities 30; context 27; and debating 93; doors of 19; environment 27, 30; experiences 31; higher 81, 103; law of 96; open 3; processes 27; requirements 27; rote 27; student 81; teaching and 25, 31, 50, 81, 103, 108; technicians of 7; way of 94
listen 93, 103; expected to 31; passively 31; willing to xii, 25
listening 47, 103

managerialism 1, 12; corporate 50; language of 1
marginalisation 39, 45, 49, 100
market viii, 71, 102; culture 66; economy 4; educational 70; financial 67; free 67, 80; global 72; international 70; national 70; neoliberal 69
marketisation 67, 68, 71
massification 1–3, 5, 6, 12, 25, 26, 29
metaphysical i, xiii, 86, 90, 101, 108; beyond 89; new xiii, 90; notions of xiii, 89; profanations xiv, 104; use 101
moral 7, 17, 90; action 39; allegiance 44; contributions 3; future 63; imperative 12; -ity 8, 63; obtuseness 69; philosophers 97; principles 18; purpose 8; responsibilities 41; value 67; world 16

needs 69; academic 3; of colonialism 103; development 49; human 69; individual 15; knowledge 49; learner 69; market 4; regional 49; society 8, 9; of society 8; student 4, 19
neoliberal: agenda 76; commodification 67; contexts x; corporatism 100; economic imperatives 71; economic

Index

revolution 72; market imperatives 69; philosophy 67; texts x
neoliberalism 66, 67; discourse of 67
neoliberalist: agenda 73; conceptions 6, 81; imperative 100; stance 73

open-mindedness 17, 40
oppression 62, 90, 100, 103

participation 2, 4; active 34; constructive 42; democratic 9, 69; systems 2
patriotism xii, 37, 43, 44; inward 43; limitation of 42; optics of 43
pedagogical: actions 82; concerns 106; encounters 4, 31; engagement 25; exclusion 83; moments 81; relations 32; spaces 76; vision 44; vulnerabilities 81; vulnerability 81, 87
pedagogical practices 3
pedagogy 2, 4, 34, 72, 81, 82, 87, 102, 118; of difference 104, xiv; of dignity xiv, 104; of discomfort xiv, 104; of dissensus 33, 34; higher 81, 82; of shame xiv, 104; teaching 25; of teaching and learning 103
performative 10; actions 54; compliance 10; demands 54; game 54; university 10, 11; ways x
performativity x, 54, 72, 89; language of 1; university x
philosophy 18, 63, 72, 85, 86; activity of 18; of critique 62; as deconstruction 19; of deconstruction 20; of essences 48; neoliberal 67; understanding of 85
Philosophy of Education 71, 72, 74
place 1, 4, 23, 31, 32, 47, 66, 72, 76, 93; of conflict 47; connected 101; of critical resistance xii, 57, 60, 64; of critique vi; of polarisation 107; separate 2; for systematic inquiry vi; of thought vi
play viii, xiv, 10, 11, 17, 25, 92–95, 98, 100, 104, 106–108; act of 94; Agamben's 98; continuous i, 108; dead 105; engage in 94; example of 92; explication of 11; idea of 10; inclination to 12; institution of i, xi; measure of viii; notion of xiv, 90; ongoing 101; perpetual ix, xiv, 100, 103, 106, 107; spheres of 92; state of 107; understanding of 11; university of xi, 9, 92, 93, 98, 100, 104, 108
playful: understanding 100; university xiv, 89, 100, 104
playfulness xiv, 90, 93, 101; act with 102
political i, 26, 28, 51, 64, 108; affairs 90; agenda 106; boundaries 64; change 47, 62; complexity 7, 55, 65; context 47; deliberations 43; dilemmas 50, 75; economy theory 67; injustices 47; innuendo 83; landscape 101; operations 91; position 75; promises 43; resistance 11, 94, 107; responsibilities 41; rhetoric 50; stability 37; task 95; theory 21; transformation 18, 67; vision 44; well-being 50
politics: democratic 33; of dissensus 35; of shame 101, 102; of truth 17
post-colonial: Africa 94, 96; teacher education 94
power vi, 20, 32, 44, 51, 57–61, 64, 91; abuse of 17; apparatuses of 91; of appropriation 64; assertion of 60; capacity 32; challenging 61; climate of 64; constructions of 103; to decide 59; deprived of 17; effects of 17; exercise of 91; in the faculty 73; idea of 17; implications of 60; -less 44, 61; limited 61; military 71; outside 17; of the people 32; relations 60; relationships of 60; resistance to 17, 59; sacred 91; of self-definition 3; structures of 20; systems of 103; techno-scientific 63; -to-say 17; -to-think-and-judge 17; of truth 17, 59; of a university 61; versions of 18; webs of 58
powerful 32, 58
profanation viii, xiv, 11, 90–92, 95, 98, 102; act of 12, 108; act with 94; conception of 98; concern of 96; connectedness to 25; of education 108; explication of 92; of higher education 108; metaphysical xiv,

104; notion of 89; quest for xi; of the sacred 11; understanding of 11; of the university viii; university in xii

protesting 18, 39, 59, 62; actions 51; appeasement 18; call to 39; engaging in 51; plans of 38; reasons for 39; risk of 39; roles in 47; students 38, 39, 47, 50, 59, 84, 97

provocation 7, 11, 64, 96, 104

public: assets 67; boundaries 51; character 37; commitment 4; concern 51; domain 68; good xiii, 50, 66; HEI 48, 51, 96; imagination 18, 67; interest 43; issues 37, 39, 75; knowledge 75; life 18, 67; mission 37, 38; responsibility xii, 37, 45, 62, 63; role 8, 9; service 40; space 62; spheres i, viii, 40, 108; things 94; use 94; values 68

rationality xiv, 101, 104

reason 7, 10, 11, 17, 18, 40, 63; chains of 94; exercise of 71; principle of 71; university of vi

reasoning: habits of xiv, 104; methodological 16

reflection 7, 10, 11, 16, 69, 91; critical vi, 69; lack of 27; meaningful 76; provocative 63; quality of 96; self- 51

reflective 63, 86; provocatively 63–65

research 70, 73, 95, 100, 108; academic 68; activities xiv, 93; applicable 71; applied 3; basic 71; benchmarking 75; capacity 75; demands 73, 76; and education 8; educational 95; employees 68; end-oriented xiii, 70, 71; engagement 95; excellence x; forms of 95; funding 75; for impact 71; -intensive environment 70; -intensive institutions 75; -intensive university 66, 101; interests 20; managers 68; outputs 20, 73, 74, 104; priority 75; productivity 6, 104, 105; profile 9; programme 68, 71; programmed 71; projects 67; publications 73; pure 3; quality 70; results 68; scholars 68; scientific 69; skills 9; stem cell 8; students 70; teaching and 5, 70; types of 102; university 5, 39, 49

researcher i, 74, 104; educational 95; generation of 74

respect 43, 66, 81, 96, 97, 102, 107; dignity and 96, 107; dis- 101; ethics of 102; for human agency 41; mutual 41, 42; for the other 106; for persons 41; possibility of 106; self- 96

responsibility vii, viii, x, xii, xiii, 8, 9, 12, 14, 20, 27, 30, 38, 39, 45, 63, 64, 89, 96, 106; civic 41; conception of 39; form of 39; human 44; idea of 38; new 62, 63; personal 67; professional 39; public xii, 37, 45, 62, 63; purpose of 8; shared 81; social 3, 40, 106; taking 8, 62; university of 39, 61, 63; wider 62

scholarship 9, 54, 69, 104, 107; academic 4; credible 76; critical 72; pursuit of 76

social 28, 51, 55; agency 18, 67; capital 59; class vii; construction 29; contexts 26; development 49, 50; dilemma 50; equity 50; exclusion 83; form of enquiry 85; groups 43; hegemony 17, 59; impact xi, 108; inequalities 2; injustices 47; issues 3; justice xi, 40, 49; landscape 76, 101; learning processes 27; mobility 2, 26; order 34; practices 27, 44; purposes 9, 49; relevance x; responsibility x, 3, 40, 106; returns 26; role 3; sciences 72, 105; stability 37, 40; standing 22; studies 72; transformation 18, 67; universe 85; welfare 9; well-being 50

sociopolitical: practice 58; relationships 58; structures 58

South Africa 5, 9, 26, 38, 42, 47, 48, 50, 59, 74, 75, 96; apartheid 54, 91; context 2, 6, 26; education 94; example 104; higher education 29, 48, 49, 74, 103; higher education sector 105; higher learning 103;

languages 84; massification 2; nationalised interests 71; needs 49; perspectives 29; post-apartheid 2, 34, 37, 72, 106; professors 104; story 54; universities 19, 37, 59, 71, 74, 96, 103, 105
space 1, 2, 9, 23, 35, 41, 76, 92, 98; communal 4; of conflict 48; of contestation 7; of deconstruction 23; of deliberation 19, 31; for democratic moments 31; for demostrating research skills 9; of disagreement 7; of dissent 48; educational 41, 44; of engagement 19, 31; head (*see* head space); of openness 17; pedagogical 76; of pedagogical engagement 26; public 62; of radical thinking 31; sacred 91; safe 34; of a university 5, 11, 26, 31, 35, 39, 42, 51, 64, 103
students i, xi, xii, 3, 4, 7, 14, 17, 19, 22, 25–35, 38–45, 47–49, 51, 52, 57–61, 63, 64, 69, 70, 72, 74, 76, 81, 83, 93, 94, 96–98, 100, 102–104, 106; access 49, 50, 55; Afrikaans-speaking 100; alienation 25, 27, 28; articulation 84; assessment 59; attachment 28; black 39, 50; bodies 3, 28, 100; calibre of 104; conduct 58; decontextualised 28; demands 67; demographics 29; disengaged 1; disruptions 32; education 49; encounters 58, 83, 102; engagement 4, 28, 31, 32, 94, 103; experience 26, 42; groups 45; higher education 26, 27; immigrant 41; innovation 94; kinds of 45, 103; knowledgeable 47; learning 81; learning experiences 31; level 10; marginalised 42; migratory patterns 29; minority-faith 41; needs 4, 19; numbers 1, 3, 4, 12, 28; outstanding 66, 101; penalty 58; population 5; postgraduate i, 73, 104; potential 60; poverty 57; privileged 42; protests 38, 39, 47, 50, 59, 84, 97; quality 94; questioning 58; reasons 51; registration 48; remote 5; research 83; retention 26; revenue 3; right to speak 32; silent 84; throughput 26; training 49; university 26, 46, 57, 62; uprising 62; voiceless 44; voices 82; vulnerability 81, 82
subversion 21; of academic programme 94; of alienation 25; of forgiveness 21; of practices xiv, 94; of traditions 94, 98, 100–102; of the university 101
subversiveness xiv, 76, 104
suspicion 8, 11, 63

teachers xi, 5, 22, 25, 28, 31–35, 40, 44, 51, 60, 62, 63, 69, 78, 81, 93, 94, 96, 102, 106; actions of 52; approach 81; authoritarian 93; authoritative 106; authority of 74; education 72, 94–96, 102; educators 96; engagement 31; first-time 95; pre-service 93, 102; prospective 95, 102; spiritual 79; student 96; university xii, 22, 25, 32, 34, 51, 63, 81, 93
teaching 29, 68, 73, 75, 83, 95, 96, 100; act of 62; approach 28, 94; and assessment 28, 93; and community 28; compassionate 81, 87; engagement 28; experts 68; jobs 5; and learning 25, 31, 50, 86, 103, 108; methodologies 94; pedagogies 25; practices 25, 45; profession 96; and research 5, 70; tasks of 3
teaching–learning 81
testimony 52, 53; bearing 53, 54; living 79
thinking i, xii, 1, 4, 9–11, 18, 19, 31, 52, 53, 55, 60, 70, 89, 95, 104; actions 52; act of 7; capacity to 57; community of 38, 63; conceptions of x; constrained 10; critical 69, 72; critique 50; cultivate 10; emphasis on x, i; exercise of 18, 22; form of 53; ideas of 20; instance of 50; institution x; institution of 14; killing 1; kind of 7; line of 52; new 17, 20, 30; plurality of 23; radical 31; renewed 11; risky 7; understanding of 51; university x, i, xi, xii, 1, 6, 8–10, 12, 14, 23, 28, 34, 37, 39–42, 45, 47, 50, 52–54, 60,

Index

63, 64, 69, 84, 89, 90, 92, 98, 103; ways of xii, 8, 25, 31, 38, 42, 51, 94, 104

thought vi, vii, viii, xii, 57, 60, 61, 76, 79, 95; critical 1, 4, 6, 72; human 29; independent 1; place of vi; provocative 76; Rumi's 79; salient 79; seminal xi, xiii, 17, 31, 76; site of vi; upheavals of 51

togetherness xiii, 84, 86, 87, 89; challenges of 103; of education x; efforts 29; epistemological 29; issues 95; political 18; social 18, 67

transformation 2, 3, 6, 102

transition 8, 26, 35, 50

trust 19, 80

truth vii, viii, xi, xii, xiii, 7, 14–20, 23, 57, 61, 86, 89, 100, 101; boundary of 58; commitment to 61; concern for xiii, 86; constructions of 20; deconstructed xiv, 23, 104; diverse 65; enactments of 20; hierarchical 23; interest in 7, 18; kinds of i, xiii, 89; knowledge and 23; our 15; own 17, 58, 64; politics of 17; power of 17, 59; pursuit of i, xiii, 14, 23, 38, 45, 61, 71, 89; regime of 17, 20, 57–60, 64, 65; relation to 14; searching for xi, xiv, 14, 20, 23, 104; seekers 68; telling the xi, 7, 14, 17–19, 22, 23; understanding 15; university of 25; versions of 18

understanding vii, viii, x, xi, xii, xiii, 11, 18, 28, 31, 33–35, 38, 69, 70, 80, 81, 85, 86, 97, 104; of community 82, 83; of compassion 81; of a concept 52; of critique 52; of deconstruction 20, 22; deeper 47; Derridian 17; of disciplinary knowledge 86; of education 96; essential 69; of God's purposes 85; of higher education 81; of higher learning 81; of influence 106; of institutional culture 29; intrinsic 86; ordinary 21; own 16; philosophical xiii, 86; of philosophy 85; of play 11; playful 100; of profanation 11; Rumi's 87; of theoretical constructs 107;

of thinking 51; universe of 16; a university 6, 10; of a university 63, 79, 100; of vulnerability 87; of witnessing 53

universities x, i, ix, vi, xi, xii, vii, xiv, viii, xiii, 1, 3–12, 14, 16–20, 22, 23, 25, 26, 28–34, 37–42, 45, 47–52, 54–55, 57–68, 70–74, 76, 78, 80, 81, 83–84, 86, 87, 89, 90, 93, 94, 98, 100–108; academics i, xi, 7; advantaged 39; African 12, 95, 102, 108; Afrikaans 100; agenda 62; antagonistic 6, 8, 10; appeal to excellence xiii; autonomy 18, 45; beyond critique vi, xiii, 47, 52, 76, 78, 79, 84, 86, 102, 106; campuses 41, 42; career 5; classroom 26; climate 73; commercialisation 68; of compassion xiii; compassionate 86; comprehensive 49; connectedness 7; contemporary 4; corporatist 6, 66, 73, 74; of critique xiv, xii, 53, 104; critique of viii, 19; cultures 28; curriculum xiv, 93; democratic (*see* democratic university); education 14, 15, 32, 34, 72, 79, 81, 82, 100–102; employees 68; entrepreneurial xiii, 10, 66–70, 76; environment 26, 35, 70; equals 35; ethics 102; ethos 99; faculty 73; fees 59, university 39; governance 50; idea of a xiv, xiii, 23, 25, 31, 84, 89, 104; identity 28; -in-becoming xiv; inertia 57; knowledge xiii, 40, 62; life xiv, 28, 35, 54, 93; of love 99; management 32, 47, 51, 68; massification 3; matters 35; mission of 33, 37–39; modern 9; neoliberal 54; notion of 76, 78, 79; operations 68; organisation of 71; performative x, 10, 11; of play i, xi, xiv, 9, 12, 98, 104, 108; playful xiv, 11, 92, 93, 100, 103, 104, 106–108; policies 32; of possibilities 8, 10; powers of 61; practices 40, 99; prestigious 5, 26; private 5; profanation of the xii, viii; professors 34; programmes 94; property 50; of reason vi; research 5, 49 (*see* research university);

research-intensive 66, 101; of responsibility 39; responsibility of a 61–63; rivalrous 9; role of 2, 4, 8, 45, 62, 98, 106; scholars xiv, 51, 94; sector 50; silence 57; social responsibility 106; South African 19, 59, 71, 74, 103; space 5, 35, 42, 51, 102; spaces 25, 39; staff 60; state of 3; structures 28, 39, 47, 50, 97; students 26, 32, 57; tasks xi, xiii, 17, 22, 44, 62, 66, 86; teachers xii, 22, 25, 32, 34, 51, 63, 81, 93; of technology 49; thinking (*see* thinking university); of thinking (*see* thinking university); of truth 25; unconditional xii, 57, 65, 103; undemocratic 31; well-being 50; without condition xii, 57, 60–62, 64, 65, 80, 102, 103; of witnessing 52, 55

violence 39, 44, 47, 81

witness: bearing xii, 52–54, 76, 108
witnessing xii, xiv, 9, 52–55, 57, 76, 84, 104, 105

For Product Safety Concerns and Information please contact our EU representative GPSR@taylorandfrancis.com
Taylor & Francis Verlag GmbH, Kaufingerstraße 24, 80331 München, Germany

www.ingramcontent.com/pod-product-compliance
Lightning Source LLC
Chambersburg PA
CBHW051752230426
43670CB00012B/2260